The Design and Development of Computer Based Instruction

J. Steven Soulier

Utah State University

Allyn and Bacon, Inc.

Boston   London   Sydney   Toronto

Library of Congress Cataloging-in-Publication Data

Soulier, J. Steven.
  The design and development of computer based instruction.

  Includes bibliographies and index.
  1. Computer-assisted instruction.   I. Title.
LB1028.5.S69   1988   371.3'9445   87-14413
ISBN 0-205-11160-2

Printed in the United States of America

10 9 8 7 6 5 4 3 2 1   91 90 89 88 87

Dedicated to the Memory of

Jared Andrew Soulier

He didn't live long enough to be part of the computer generation.
But he taught all who knew him the meaning of life.

Contents

Preface

It has been said that we live in the midst of an information revolution during which computers are changing not only the way we live but the way we think. There is no doubt that the computer has already changed the way we do business and entertain ourselves. We even see signs that the computer is changing the way we learn and what we learn. Computer literacy, a catch-word just a few years ago, is now an accepted term, part of the curriculum in education and industry. Certainly, there are more pieces of computer hardware being used now in teaching and learning than ever before; but has the computer really improved matters? The hardware industry can't provide the answer; those who develop computer based instruction courseware must do so.

Now that the infatuation is wearing off, we realize that the computer is just another tool; how useful it is depends on what people do with it. In the hands of a master, a hammer and chisel create a masterpiece; in the hands of a fool, they are tools of destruction. So it is with the computer. If used properly, it can change the way we teach in many positive ways; but, if it is to realize its full potential for computer based instruction, it must have a creative instructional sound design.

This is a book of guidelines and suggestions drawn from the author's own experience in designing CBI materials and the experience of numerous others. Whether you are a professional or a nonprofessional CBI developer, it should start you off in the right direction. The guidelines are presented within a systematic structure. Many professional developers have found that this format, when fully applied, improves the quality of instruction.

Each stage of the development process builds on the previous stage. In some CBI program development, it takes only a few hours to carry out all the stages described. Others may require weeks, months, and even years, of planning and developing before a final product is delivered to the market. You will have to decide what needs to be done and what doesn't. Allow enough time to realize your, and the computer's, fullest potential.

We are still in the process of finding out just what the potential of CBI really is. This book is simply a collection of ideas and past and present experiences. Your own ideas may be better. Try them out; share your results with others. I am continually looking for new ideas and new approaches to improve the use of computers in instruction. If you have any you want to share with me, I would appreciate hearing from you.

ACKNOWLEDGMENTS

My thanks to Alan Hofmeister, Ron Thorkildsen, and Larry Possey for their assistance, both in reviewing drafts and in suggesting changes.

To Harvey Frye, who never touched a computer but who became my mentor in so many other ways; to Bob Woolley for getting me started with the computer and for supporting my computer habit all these years; and to Bruce Tognazzini, who was one of the first people to really understand what computer/human interface really meant, and to do something about it.

To my colleagues in the Department of Instructional Technology at Utah State University, who took on additional responsibilities to allow me the time to work on the book.

To Diana Gibney, who did an excellent job copy editing the manuscript.

A special thanks to my wife, Janet, for reviewing drafts and for getting me through the highs and lows of writing, and to Ryan, Aimee, and Megan, the generation that continues to teach me what computers, and their potential, are all about.

J. Steven Soulier

1

Systematic Design of Computer Based Instruction

It's not the things we don't know that get us into trouble; it's the things we do know that ain't so.

Will Rogers

1.0 INTRODUCTION

Designing and developing computer based instructional courseware is a process requiring a great deal of planning and patience. Few computer based courseware packages are ever developed by a single individual. Typically, resources are drawn from a variety of professions. This results in a team effort that involves content experts, instructional designers, writers, programmers, artists, evaluators, and other specialists from related fields. Where most new courseware designers get in trouble is in not realizing the complexity of the task they are undertaking. Some assume that, because they are a good programmer, they can write any kind of computer program. Others assume that knowing a content area is enough to get them by. Rare is the individual who has all the skills necessary to develop a complete courseware package. Even he, or she, needs others—as a sounding board for ideas.

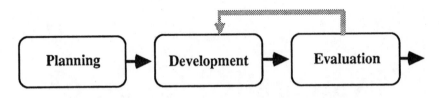

Figure 1.1   CBI development stages

Good ideas don't result automatically in a good program. They are only a starting point. The most dangerous thing a courseware designer can do when he or she gets an idea is to immediately sit down in front of a computer and begin to program. The creation of an effective courseware package requires careful planning and design, which should take as much as 70 percent of the total effort. Taking the time to plan results in a more effective program. In addition, time and money are saved during the final development stages.

Planning is something most of us do every day of our lives. Almost everything we do comes out better if we take the time to plan. A young child's planning may be directed at something as basic as how to get a cookie from the cookie jar, while an adult's plans may involve something as complex as determining the necessary steps for landing a probe on Mars. It is hard to imagine what a new house would end up looking like if we didn't start out with some type of plan or blueprint before we laid the foundation. Sometimes our planning is kept inside our head; at other times we make a hard copy of our plans so that others can see how we, or they, are supposed to proceed.

When applied to the design of instruction, this planned, systematic approach is usually referred to as *instructional design & development*, or I.D. & D. There have been numerous books written on the subject of instructional design and development. Many are listed in the reference section at the end of this chapter. It is recommended that the reader obtain one or more of these books to gain additional ideas on the general instructional design process.

Instructional design can be broken down into three stages (as shown in Figure 1.1). The first stage is the *planning stage*. The

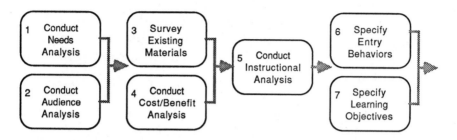

Figure 1.2   CBI planning stages

purpose is to answer the basic questions: who? what? and why? Stage two is the *development stage*. This stage focuses on the questions of how? and where? It provides for the actual production of the courseware. The third stage is an *evaluation stage*, where both formal and informal evaluation is undertaken and where, through revision loops, a product may be redesigned and reproduced numerous times until it lives up to the designer's expectations.

The three stages may only take a few minutes of a developer's time and thought. Or they may take as long as several weeks or months, involving a design team and volumes of written documents. It depends on the complexity of the project. In either case, applying a systematic, planned approach to the design of interactive computer based instruction has been shown to save time, effort, and money. The end product is more professional and effective, and it has a higher probability of meeting its desired purposes.

1.1   PLANNING STAGE

The seven steps of the planning stage are illustrated in Figure 1.2. The first four steps help you determine if the project you are about to undertake is needed, worthwhile, and appropriate for a computer based application. The next three steps help you specify the tasks and objectives to be covered by the program.

For some programs, it is possible to complete these steps by mentally answering the seven questions listed below. If, as you ask yourself each question, the answer isn't readily apparant, then you may want to follow the more detailed processes described in other sections of this chapter.

1. What does my intended audience already know, what should they know, and therefore what needs to be taught (general instructional goals)?
2. What characteristics do my intended audiences share that will help or hinder their learning the desired materials?
3. Are there any instructional materials available that can either teach or be used to support the teaching of the needed information?
4. Is it really worth all the time and effort I am about to put into the project, even if the need does exist?
5. What specific information or skills (tasks) do students need to learn to reach my instructional goal?
6. Which of these tasks does the student need to learn from some other source or in some other way before starting my program?
7. What are my specific learning objectives?

1.2   NEEDS ANALYSIS

A needs analysis is meant to help you determine what your intended audience already knows or is already able to perform and what they should know or should be able to perform. Once you have identified the discrepancies between the two, you will have a general idea of what concepts and skills (general instructional goals) your computer program should teach.

The first step is to recognize that a problem or a need exists. You do this through personally observing learners, conducting surveys and formal interviews with employers or past students, and/or reading articles describing broader local or national problems. Some instructional problems are very specific. For example some learners are unable to perform up to criteria on their seven-times tables. Other instructional problems are more general; such as the failure of learners to think logically.

In order to know whether an instructional problem really exists, you need two pieces of information. First, you must define what the desired performance ought to be. Second, you must know what the present performance of your intended audience is.

Defining desired performance

Desired performance may be based on some type of national or local norm, or on expectations set by an individual teacher, by the learner, or by management. The source of the desired performance is not nearly as important as its relevance to long-range outcomes. Desired performance should be described as specific performance-behaviors that can be compared with a learner's present performance.

At this stage, always look at an area of desired performance that is larger than the area you are prepared to handle with your intended program. Some desired performances may already be known by the target audience, while others may not be appropriate for a computer based approach. The fact that an organization has established a set of desired performances does not necessarily mean that it needs the instructional materials to teach them.

An example of a desired performance may be a statement taken from a set of guidelines for computer literacy of preservice teachers:

> All preservice teachers will be able to demonstrate the proper use, operation, and care of a computer and a variety of peripheral equipment, such as a: diskette, disk and tape drive, printer, monitor, modem, light pen, multiplexer, graphics tablet, and scanner.

In industry, a desired set of performances might be taken from a job description:

Be able to conduct an internal review of all components of the system, and conduct a pretest and formal test of the system before it is delivered to the customer.

Designers should, of course, be concerned with the validity and reliability of statements of desired performance, but they should not attempt to change them based upon their own personal biases.

Defining present performance

Present performance may be defined in terms of interviews, test scores, observations, or by analysis by qualified personnel. In any case, it should be described in specific performance-behavioral terms that can be compared with desired or future performance. For example:

The average student currently gets 45 percent of all story problems correct.

or

Students of this age level currently have an attention span of from 3 to 5 minutes.

Determining the present performance of your target audience should not be done in a haphazard manner. The most effective way of preventing this is to develop a questionnaire or checklist containing the specific performances you are interested in. Figure 1.3 illustrates this approach.

Identifying performance discrepancies

When both present and desired performance are known, you are ready to evaluate the discrepancies between the two. A three-column table similar to the one shown below is often effective in performing the analysis. The discrepancies you find should fairly accurately indicate your instructional problems.

Performance   observation   checklist

Yes No

1. Do employees know what materials will be required to do a job?

2. Can they locate the necessary materials quickly?

3. Do they understand their roles and assignments?

4. Do they seem to waste time getting ready to work?

5. Do they use the tools properly?

6. Do they care for the tools properly?
Comments:

Figure 1.3   Sample performance observation checklist

Present Performance	Desired Performance	Discrepancy Analysis
Current reading rate 150 WPM	State average 235 WPM	85 WPM slower than state average
Average student reads 3.5 books per quarter	School average 5.6 books per quarter	Our students read 2.1 fewer books than the average student
Students have difficulty coming up with logical solutions to problems	Logical problem solving is an objective of the state curriculum	Students don't know how to solve problems logically

Recognizing that a problem might exist does not necessarily imply that the problem is important or that a cure is possible or feasible given certain cost, time, or other constraints. It has been suggested that "there must be a lot of hypochondriacs among developers because there are so many programs designed to solve problems where no real problem exists." Like doctors, instructional designers need to learn how to recognize real problems from "pet projects" and the "illness" from its symptoms.

Writing a problem statement

The problem statement does *not* describe what needs to be done to solve the problem or to cure any of the symptoms. It simply focuses attention on the specific characteristics of the problem itself. The following is an example of what a problem statement might look like:

Problem Statement:

Students are unable to analyze story problems for essential information. This results from:
a failure to identify pertinent information,
a failure to organize information logically, and
a failure to utilize all necessary information.

Stating an instructional goal

When you understand the problem and its major symptoms, you can state an instructional goal that accurately describes what learners should be able to know, do, or feel, once they have completed your program. The following is an example:

Upon completion of this courseware package:

"Given a set of story problems, the learner will be able to, with 90% accuracy, analyze those problems for essential information and solve them by accurately identifying, organizing, and utilizing pertinent information."

An instructional goal, even though general in nature, should describe the final performance learners will be expected to demonstrate when they complete the program, and the condition under which that performance will be evaluated.

1.3   AUDIENCE ANALYSIS

Describing instructional needs provides important information about what should be presented in a courseware package; but it is equally important to understand your audience, those for whom you are designing the courseware. To help you identify these critical characteristics, you need to perform an audience analysis. You need to determine which characteristics will help and which will hinder their ability to learn, or to overcome the identified instructional problem.

Too often, audience analyses focus on irrelevant information like age, sex, race, previous grades in school, and so on. While these are sometimes useful, more often, they serve to inaccurately stereotype individuals. The following information is of far greater interest to the instructional designer:

1. *Entry knowledge and skills.* Does the intended audience have the prerequisite knowledge and skills to handle the pro-

posed instruction? Your analysis should permit you to specifically describe the relevant knowledge and skills they lack, including math, reading, and vocabulary levels, along with specific skills related to the proposed program content. Careful analysis of what your intended audience already knows helps you avoid using up limited computer memory and learner time for unnecessary instruction.

2. *Social and cultural background.* Does the learner's background include specific social or cultural experiences that will help you present meaningful examples that will tie new information to past experience? Are there standardized symbols, signs, and metaphors that your audience understands, and that can be used to make instruction more efficient?

3. *Cognitive development level.* What level of abstraction might be meaningful, and what is the learner's current attention span for new information? What verbal and visual literacy skills does the learner possess, and how do these skills effect your presentation of new information via the computer?

4. *Physical perception abilities.* Does the learner have a handicap that might hinder the reception of the proposed message, such as color blindness, lack of manual dexterity, or a hearing or reading problem? Does the intended user have any special aptitudes that can be used to aid receptivity, such as a particular cognitive style favoring sight or sound?

5. *Personal interests and goals.* What kinds of things are your learners interested in? Knowing their interests will help you select activities and examples. What motivates them? Are they best motivated by internal interests? Or do they generally require some type of external encouragement, like preparing for a test or working for a reward?

6. *Attitudes, biases, and prejudices.* Are there attitudes that must be dealt with before learning can take place? For example, learners who are afraid of computers often have difficulty learning from computer based materials. Do the learners have certain convictions and biases? These can be used to select or avoid examples or to help motivate the learner.

7. *Individual time and resource constraints.* How much time can the learner spend with the materials? Many computer based programs are developed without consideration for the limitations of the individual learning environment. Individual resources such as student time, students per computer, type and availability of computers, disk drives and other peripheral devices, along with other resource considerations, may play an important part in how you design your program. Include it in your analysis of your intended audience.

8. *Computer background, knowledge, and experience.* Since the computer will be the delivery system for the instruction, it is extremely important for you to know the computer literacy level of the target audience. As you already know, to load and startup a computer program requires a few special skills. Your audience need not be literate in all aspects of computers, only those that directly effect their ability to load and operate your program as you intend.

Like the needs assessment discussed earlier, it is useful to formalize your audience analysis. Develop a questionnaire or a worksheet listing specific things you think you should know about your target audience and the environment in which they will be learning and functioning. Use it to guide your interviews with representatives from the intended audience, as well as with parents, employers, teachers, psychologists, managers, and others who work with them.

It is not essential to know everything about every audience. In step 2, conducting an audience analysis, always refer back to the specific instructional problem and goal you developed in step 1 (see Figure 1.2). The purpose of an audience analysis is to help you further clarify what and who you will be working with. The audience analysis should help you identify those characteristics of the learner, both strengths and weaknesses, that are critical to the learning process and that impact on how you design the program.

1.4   SURVEY EXISTING MATERIALS

Even though you know what the instructional needs are and who the intended audience is, you should not proceed with the development of the program until you have asked yourself, Why am I undertaking this project? Don't take this question lightly. To develop one hour of interactive computer based material requires an estimated 100 to 500 hours. Developers should never undertake a project unless the potential use and impact of the program justifies the investment.

One justification is clear—a demonstrated need on a broad local or national scale in an area in which there are no adequate materials available to overcome the problem. Survey current instructional materials. Include books, films, audio tapes, and other media as well as computer based materials. Review media catalogs, curriculum guides, advertisements from commercial companies, and *Books in Print*. Look for resources that solve the identified instructional problem, as well as those that might be used to support your potential computer based courseware. Survey other teachers or colleagues. Many times they are aware of resources you might have missed.

Few instructional problems can be solved by a single computer program. If you can identify other outstanding materials, and then design your computer program to fill in the gaps, you may cut your development time by half or more, and with highly effective results. With recent advancements in computer based interactive video tape and videodisc, it is highly likely that such cross media packages will tie in with current concepts of computer based or computer assisted instruction.

1.5   COST-BENEFIT ANALYSIS

Once the developer is sure that the product is really needed, he or she must determine whether it is the best, most cost-effective solution to the problem. Both steps are prerequisite to the development of computer programs.

Determining cost effectiveness

All too often, educational decisions are made on the basis of cost alone. If an instructional package costs under fifty dollars we buy it, or we develop it, but if it costs over a thousand dollars we don't even consider it. It is true that most businesses and educational organizations don't have money to spend on expensive instructional packages; however, it is equally true that some fifty dollar packages are a waste of money. Cost is only one factor in determining the *cost* effectiveness of a product. Other factors include:

1. How often, and by how many individuals, will the materials be used? The cost of a program used by one learner once a year may be very expensive at $100. The same program, when used by 100 or more learners throughout the year, may work out to one dollar or less per learner and therefore be highly cost effective. If this same program is used for as long as 10 years at this rate, the actual cost may be reduced to as little as ten cents per learner. Developers generally should not consider developing programs to solve the problems of a single learner or even a specific group of learners. The value of a computer based program is its ability to be used again and again. Cost divided by use (e.g., cost per student, per contact hour, or per work station) gives a much more accurate assessment of the real cost of computer based materials.
2. Is the product marketable? Many times an individual teacher, business, or educational organization can recoup some of their investment in developing computer based training materials by selling programs to others who have the same need. Does your needs assessment suggest that the problem you have identified has broad local or national

implications? If so, design your program to make it more transportable. Begin by immediately contacting software distributors who may be willing to market your program. If none exists, you might want to suggest that your organization, business, or state set up a consortium of instructional software developers for this purpose. While not an inexpensive undertaking, the Minnesota Educational Computing Consortium (MECC) has provided a cost-effective model. States and businesses with large investments in development might consider such an alternative.

3. Is the computer the most appropriate medium for presentation? This is perhaps the most important question you should ask yourself before you proceed with developing a courseware package. Computers, despite their many unique contributions, are no panacea for instruction. Later in the book we will discuss design techniques that will help you make use of some of the computer's unique qualities. For now, ask yourself if what you hope to teach could be better taught using a book (don't make the computer an electronic page turner), an animated film, a programmed text, or some other more cost-effective medium. Make a list of the unique contributions you believe the computer provides, to help solve the identified instructional problem. If unique qualities are in short supply, then consider another medium. Computers are still relatively expensive and are found in limited numbers in most schools and businesses, so don't put your presentation on the computer just because you like computers. Make sure it requires a high level of interaction and that the use of the computer is fully justified.

4. What are the indirect and long-term costs going to be? Can you make some type of estimate of the cost of computer hardware for both the development and the effective implementation of your proposed program? What are the continuing costs in hardware and software maintenance, student aids and lab monitors, consumables (e.g., paper,

diskettes, printer ribbons), furniture, and other classroom furnishings?

5. What are the real benefits to be derived from the courseware when it is completed? Can you increase the instructional effectiveness, or reduce instructional costs while being at least as effective? Can you reduce teaching time? Can you increase productivity or reduce time lost on a job? Can you motivate nonmotivated learners? Can you teach difficult concepts more easily, or can you teach new content that could not have been taught without the help of the computer? Can you increase learner retention? Can you decrease teacher load?

Comparing real *costs* with apparent *benefits* gives you a pretty good indication of whether you should continue with the project or not.

If your idea doesn't appear to have a positive cost/benefit ratio, don't give up. The need for high quality computer based instructional materials is great, and the market is wide open. It would pay to identify a new need, one worthy of your personal investment.

Personal benefit analysis

Your personal investment is something you should consider before you begin. As mentioned earlier, developing a program is generally no small task. List your commitments to the project, and write down what you expect to get out of writing the program. Commitments include such things as:

Time. Remember, this probably isn't the only thing you have to work on.

Budget. If you are going to have to hire a programmer or a graphic artist, or even purchase disks and paper for printing out documentation, or stamps for mailing questionnaires, or pay to advertise your program, do you have enough financial backing to support the project until the first copies are sold?

Personal knowledge.   Do you already know everything you need to know to develop the program, or are you going to have to spend additional time getting ready?

Equipment support.   Your program will eventually be programmed on some pieces of equipment and will use some programming language. Do you already have all the necessary equipment and programming language, or will you have access to the equipment when the time comes?

Outside support.   All of us need help when we begin a project of this type. Do you have the support of your company, school, friends, and other organizational groups so that you can get questions answered when they need to be answered? Being a member of a computer user group, or a technical support group, can be of tremendous help throughout the final development stages.

The above commitments are not meant to scare you off, only to warn you. Enter the project already aware of what you are and are not capable of finishing. Balance commitments with what you expect to get out of developing a program. No need to spend hours developing something unique just to solve a single student's learning problem. Getting a raise or a promotion, seeing a program of your own creation sold nationally, or fulfilling a personal desire to contribute something useful may all be things that you personally expect to get out of writing a program. It doesn't really matter what your reason is. But make sure it is good enough to motivate you to complete the project.

1.6   SUMMARY

The systematic approach to interactive computer based design is a three-stage process consisting of a planning stage, a development stage, and an evaluation/revision stage.

The planning stage is a seven-step process. The first three steps help you determine if a project is needed, worthwhile, and appropriate. The final four steps help you specify the tasks and objectives your program will need to fulfill, and the anticipated entry behavior the learner will already have developed.

A needs analysis is a process used to define desired performance, define present performance, and describe discrepancies between the two. Once discrepancies are identified, the problem should be stated and the symptoms which are impacted by the problem listed and organized into a general instructional goal.

Identifying the critical characteristics of the target audience is the goal of an audience analysis. The target audience should be analyzed on such things as:

* Entry knowledge and skills
* Social and cultural background
* Cognitive development
* Physical perception abilities and preference
* Personal interests and goals
* Attitudes, bias, and prejudice
* Time and resource constraints
* Computer background

Before a decision is made to go ahead and develop a courseware package, a survey of existing materials should be done. Developers need to determine if similar material already exists that will accomplish the same instructional goal. A decision should also be made on the real cost and benefits that will result from proceeding with the development. A cost-benefit ratio should be developed, based on:

* Material and development costs
* Cost per anticipated user
* Marketability
* Availability of less expensive resources
* Usable life expectancy
* Long-term maintenance costs

- Real benefits to be derived
- Personal costs and benefits for the developer

This chapter has described a few tools for determining: (1) if a computer based program should be developed, (2) what the major instructional goal of the program ought to be, and (3) if the cost-benefit ratio is positive, suggesting that the outcome of the program is worth all the effort required to develop the courseware package.

1.7 ISSUES AND ACTIVITIES

1. Identify a potential area for CBI development and locate an authoritative source or sources where you can get a definition of the desired performances that relate to that area. Develop a checklist or questionnaire containing desired performances that seem appropriate to solve with a CBI courseware package.
2. Select a target audience and conduct a present performance interview or survey to determine the current performance level on a set of desired performance goals.
3. Perform a discrepancy analysis and develop a problem statement showing both the identified problems and the related symptoms. Develop a performance based instructional goal which describes the final performance and conditions for performance.
4. Identify a target population; determine the audience characteristics that will impact your program. Analyze and interview a segment of the target population, or conduct a literature review to find out as much as you can about the relevant characteristics of that audience. Develop the information into a written audience profile.
5. Do a cost-benefit analysis for your program.

6. Prepare a list of constraints which you personally would have if you decide to develop a courseware package.

1.8 REFERENCES

Bass, R. K., & Dills, C. R. (eds.). *Instructional Development: The State of the Art. II.* Dubuque, IA: Kendall/Hunt Publishing Co., 1984.

Burton, J. K., & Merrill, P. F. Needs assessment: Goals, needs, and priorities. In L. J. Briggs (ed.), *Instructional Design: Principles and Applications.* Englewood Cliffs, NJ: Educational Technology Publications, 1977.

Briggs, L. J. (ed.). *Instructional Design: Principles and Applications.* Englewood Cliffs, NJ: Educational Technology Publications, 1981.

Briggs, L. J., & Wager, W. W. *Handbook of Procedures for the Design of Instruction* (2nd ed.). Englewood Cliffs, NJ: Educational Technology Publications, 1977.

Craig, R. L. (ed.). *Training and Development Handbook: A Guide to Human Resource Development.* New York: McGraw-Hill, 1976.

Davies, I. K. *Competency Based Learning: Technology, Management and Design.* New York: McGraw-Hill, 1973.

Davies, I. K. *Instructional Technique.* New York: McGraw-Hill, 1981.

Dick, W., & Carey, L. *The Systematic Design of Instruction.* Glenview, IL: Scott, Foresman & Co., 1985.

Gagné, R. M. *The Conditions of Learning* (4th ed.). New York: Holt, Rinehart & Winston, 1985.

Gagné, R. M., & Briggs, L. J. *Principles of Instructional Design.* New York: Holt, Rinehart & Winston, 1978.

Kaufman, R. A. *Needs Assessment: What It Is and How to Do It.* San Diego, CA: University Consortium on Instructional Development and Technology, 1976.

Kaufman, R. A. (ed.). Special issue: Needs assessment. *Educational Technology, 17*(11)(1977).

Kaufman, R. A., & English, F. W. *Needs Assessment: Concept and Application.* Englewood Cliffs, NJ: Educational Technology Publications, 1979.

Kemp, J. E. *Instructional Design: A Plan for Unit and Course Development* (2nd ed.). Belmont, CA: Fearon Publishers, 1977.

Mager, R. F. *Goal Analysis.* Belmont, CA: Fearon Publishers, 1972.

Markle, S. *Designs for Instructional Designers*. Champaign, IL: Stipes, 1978.
Romiszowski, A. J. *Designing Instructional Systems*. New York: Kogan Page, 1984.
Rossett, A. A typology for generating needs assessments. *Journal of Instructional Development*, 6(1)(1982):28–33.

2

Conducting an Analysis of Instruction

Design informs even the simplest structure, whether of brick and steel or of prose. You raise a pup tent from one sort of vision, a cathedral from another. . . . The first principle of composition, therefore, is to foresee or determine the shape of what is to come and pursue that shape.

William Strunk and E. B. White

2.0 INTRODUCTION

Defining a general instructional problem and/or goal provides our design with its final destination; determining what needs to be done in order to get to there is the function of the instructional analysis. An instructional analysis is used to identify and sequence the essential skills, knowledge, attitudes, and events which are required to reach an instructional goal in the most efficient and effective way possible.

The process of analyzing a goal—to determine the subordinate steps required to meet that goal—is not unique to the instructional process. Professionals in business, industry, engineering, and sci-

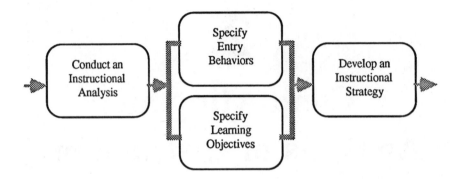

Figure 2.1   Instructional analysis

ence have used similar processes to make their work more efficient and to help them accomplish goals previously not thought possible.

The purpose for conducting an instructional analysis is to help you identify the subordinate information and skills that will make up your courseware package, to establish specific performance objectives which can be tested as the program proceeds, and to identify an instructional strategy appropriate for the learner and the desired learning outcome. Figure 2.1 illustrates the development stages to be covered in this process.

2.1   PERFORMING AN INSTRUCTIONAL ANALYSIS

Once you are satisfied that the development of an interactive computer program is the best, most cost-effective way to solve the instructional problem for the intended audience, you are ready to determine the specific subtasks or subobjectives the learner must be able to perform in order to achieve your more general instructional goal. The process of analyzing, defining, and sequencing subtasks is called "Instructional Analysis." The type of tasks being analyzed range from a job skill to an information processing or cognitive processing task.

Job performance task analysis

A performance task analysis is used to identify the steps (subtasks) performed in order to complete a particular job or skill. It is usually the easiest type of instructional analysis to perform. The most common approach is to find someone who has mastered a task, observe them carefully, and list all of the steps the individual goes through in performing that particular task. In addition to observing what a person does outwardly, it is also essential to identify the knowledge and psychomotor skills they had to have available in order to complete the task. A performance task analysis doesn't relate only to things we do at work. It can also be used to break down subtasks for skills like riding a bike, playing the guitar, or operating a computer.

An analysis of the subtasks required to manually operate a particular brand of slide projector indicated that the user had to be able to:

1. Set the mode selector.
2. Insert the slide tray.
3. Locate and attach the remote control unit.
4. Press the "FWD" button.
5. Adjust the elevation leg.
6. Move the projector until the frame is the desired size.
7. Adjust the FOCUS switch to bring the image into sharp focus.
8. Remove the slide tray after all the slides have been shown.

An analysis of the tasks required to operate the same projector in "automatic" mode included some of the same subtasks, but it also included some totally unique tasks.

Task analysis has sometimes been called "cookbook" analysis because the result is usually a step-by-step recipe for accomplishing a particular goal.

Not all instructional goals relate to observable skills. Many instructional analyses involve describing the processing of intangible information, concepts, and ideas. Performing an instructional analysis on these types of tasks may be more difficult, but not impossible. For example, here is a list of subtasks for getting the sum of four numbers:

1. Make a list of the 4 numbers.
2. Add the first number in the list to the second number; the result is called the sum.
3. Add the third number to the sum; the result is the new sum.
4. Add the fourth number to the sum; the result is the total.
5. Report the total.

Conducting an analysis of a concept and other non-job performance based skills can sometimes best be accomplished by looking at the inputs (information and skills) required for meeting the final instructional goal and then working backwards. For example, to determine which subconcepts a learner would need to understand before they can be taught the concept of Ohm's Law, begin by analyzing what inputs the concept of Ohm's Law requires. In this instance you might discover that the concept involves other concepts like electrical current, resistance, and potential difference. If you analyze these concepts you will discover that each requires certain kinds of input or preestablished knowledge. When you run out of prerequisite concepts or skills, you should have a list of all the subtasks required before someone can understand the concept of Ohm's Law.

Cognitive behavior analysis

There is a tendency in job performance task analysis to define only the most basic knowledge and applications skills used in performing a given task. It is sometimes useful to expand the performance analysis by taking a closer look at the cognitive behaviors required by a given task or goal. In this analysis, subordinate subtasks are related together and analyzed according to developmental levels of difficulty. For those not familiar with this technique of analysis, it is suggested that they read one of the references listed at the end of this chapter. In general, the central

BEHAVIOR	KNOW.	COMP.	APPL.	ANAL.	SYNT.	EVAL.
Task 1. List the elementary rules of usage.	x					
2. Differentiate between proper and improper use of pronouns.				x		
3. Indicate where commas need to be placed in complex sentences.		x				
4. Organize topics into an article.					x	
5. Use the active voice in writing.			x			
6. Select orthodox spelling.						
7. Simplify an awkward sentence.	x					
8. Criticize the style of writing used in a newspaper article.				x		x

Figure 2.2   Cognitive analysis for improving writing style

purpose of a cognitive analysis is to organize skills and subtasks according to intellectual complexity rather than job performance. The rationale behind this is that less complex behaviors are easier to learn and that, before a learner can develop behaviors that are higher on the complexity scale, they first must master those at the lower levels. The chart shown in Figure 2.2 shows the results of a partial cognitive analysis for improving a learner's writing style. The categories of cognitive skills used in this example are based on those developed by B. S. Bloom (1956) and his associates.

The results of the analysis shown in Figure 2.2 indicate that, since knowledge requires the lowest level of intellectual behavior, the learner should first be taught to "List the elementary rules of usage" and to "Select orthodox spelling" before proceeding to any other part of the lesson. Once the learner has mastered these two knowledge level skills, they can proceed to skills requiring comprehension, application, and so on. Only when they have been taught all the lower levels should they be required to "Criticize the style of writing used in a newspaper article," since this requires the highest level of cognitive skill.

Describing tasks and subtasks

Some of the subtasks listed in the above examples may not describe the steps you would follow to achieve a specific goal, but if the task or concept can be performed or understood by following these steps, the analysis is said to be **COMPLETE**. That is, all of the steps necessary to perform the task are present.

The goal of a good instructional analysis is to ensure that all necessary steps are included, and to find the most efficient and effective way of achieving a given task or goal. Sometimes, in an effort to make programs efficient, we leave out important subtasks that cause learners unnecessary problems.

For example, the addition subtasks described earlier did not provide more than a general subtask to handle the situation where the numbers or sums contain more than a single digit. In the example shown below, is the number 5 added to the number 1 or the number 2 above it?

$$\begin{array}{r} 1\ 2 \\ 5 \\ \hline ? \end{array}$$

The answer is simple enough for someone experienced in addition, but for new learners, the failure to include a subtask that teaches the child how to handle numbers having two or more digits could cause the child to fail to achieve the final learning task or objective.

In addition to being COMPLETE, a good instructional analysis should describe subtasks which are:

- FINITE, each subtask having a specified beginning point and ending point, or input and output.
- UNAMBIGUOUS, where each subtask can only be read and interpreted in one way.
- OPERATIONAL, where each subtask tells specifically what the learner needs to do or know in order to complete the subtask, and what the specific output of the task will be.

To perform an instructional analysis, begin by asking, What must a person be able to do or know in order to demonstrate competency on the desired instructional goal? Be careful not to focus the analysis too narrowly. If in the process of multiplication the learner will have to know something about carrying, or decimal places, include it as one of the subtasks. If special conditions exist which impact on a subtask, describe those conditions for later reference; e.g., "Carry the number unless adding the last column of numbers."

Check the analysis for completeness by asking "what if" questions for each subtask; e.g. "What if the water never boils?"; "What if the third number is a negative number?"; or "What if the learner can't tell time?"

When doing an instructional analysis that will later be turned into a computer based instructional program, you are better off listing too many subtasks rather than too few. You may end up not teaching all of the subtasks you identify; however, including them in the instructional analysis will help you identify possible points where learning failure may occur. Be sure to include subtasks dealing with new vocabulary or other skills required to accurately transmit or communicate the proposed skill or knowledge.

2.2 WRITING PERFORMANCE OBJECTIVES

Once you know all the tasks and subtasks which are required to meet a specific instructional goal, it is useful to describe each as a specific performance objective that will be required of the learner. A performance objective should always describe what the learner will be expected to know, do, or feel when the instructional process has been completed. Performance objectives do not describe what a CBI program will be doing, or what you will be doing as you develop the courseware package. Instead, they describe the kind of performance which the CBI program will be attempting to produce in the learner. They are used as the basis for selecting course content and instructional strategies and for evaluating learner progress.

Robert Mager made popular the concept of performance or behavior objectives in the early sixties. He suggests that objectives should include three elements:

- *Behavior*—the skill or task identified in the instructional analysis.
- *Condition*—those conditions of the instructional or actual environment that will prevail while the learner performs the task.
- *Standard*—the criteria that will be used to evaluate the performance of the learner.

A performance objective that might be appropriate to learning the above components would read:

Given a list of 5 objectives *(the condition)* the learner will be able to identify the three components suggested by Mager *(the behavior)* with 100% accuracy *(the standard)*.

The condition element should clarify the expected performance by indicating both the helping and limiting conditions that will exist while the learner is demonstrating mastery of the task. The following are examples of condition statements:

Given a broken down car...
Given a standard set of tools...
Without the aid of any reference materials...
Working on a snow-covered mountain...

The key portion of a behavior or performance objective is the action verb. The verb should specify a measurable action or behavior which the learner will be expected to perform. Verbs like understand, like, know, etc., are not verbs that describe specific behaviors. The verbs you select should reflect the intellectual and/or behavioral skill you expect the learner to develop. Figure 2.3 lists acceptable action verbs that relate to the performances defined in Bloom's (1956) taxonomy of cognitive behaviors.

LEVEL	ASSOCIATED PERFORMANCE VERBS			
KNOWLEDGE	list state write	define name identify	repeat label reproduce	recognize underline measure
COMPREHENSION	describe justify select	indicate represent explain	illustrate formulate judge	translate classify contrast
APPLICATION	apply classify select	construct solve rate	perform write use	categorize predict select
ANALYSIS	identify conclude design	criticize compare justify	resolve separate distinguish	assess locate interpret
SYNTHESIS	restate create design	combine argue organize	derive generalize formulate	write summarize predict
EVALUATION	conclude judge justify	attack avoid select	choose defend appraise	evaluate recognize identify
APPRECIATION	notice be attentive to concentrate on		show interest in show appreciation exhibit a preference	

Figure 2.3   Performance verbs for Bloom's taxonomy

Many people consider the standard, the third element of Mager's objectives, optional. If included, it should define a reasonable level of acceptable performance. The reasonable nature of a standard should be based on what will be expected when the task is performed in the actual environment. Since it will be up to the computer in most cases to decide whether a learner has mastered a skill at the intended level, it is useful if the standard can be stated in a form that the computer will be able to handle. Standards may be stated as numeric scores, proportions, percentages, logical comparisons, or exact item comparisons.

The following objectives are written according to Mager's format, and the standard associated with each could be judged by a computer:

- *Given a compound algebraic equation and without any outside help, the learner will solve the equation with 100% accuracy.*
- *Using a word processor, the learner will write a short article which contains no misspelled words and contains less than 150 words.*
- *Presented with a group of sentences, the learner will identify verb tense for each sentence.*

The wording of instructional objectives is not nearly as important as the ability of the objective to communicate to you, the learner, and others on the development team, what is expected. Let development team members, colleagues, and especially members of your target audience read over your objectives when you have finished writing them. Have them explain what they think the objective is telling them. If your understanding and their understanding of the objective don't match, rewrite them until they do. It is important that you not proceed with developing a courseware package until agreement can be reached on what the intended outcome of the package will be.

2.3   THE INSTRUCTIONAL SEQUENCE

WHEN something is taught may be as important as WHAT is taught. Trying to teach a young child an advanced mathematical principle is generally a futile effort. Not because the objective is bad or wrong but because the learner is simply not ready for that level of learning. Learners may not be ready for a particular piece of instruction for many reasons. They may lack the necessary cognitive development; they may lack a critical prerequisite concept or skill; or they may have a more specific learning problem. Whatever the reason, proper instructional sequencing is part of the solution.

The needs analysis discussed in Chapter 1 allows you to identify a single instructional goal for the program you are developing. The instructional analysis enables you to write specific performance objectives describing each basic behavior learners should be able to demonstrate when they finish working with your program. Keep this instructional goal, and the related performance objectives, in front of you during all remaining stages of development, so that you don't forget where the program is headed.

Developing an appropriate instructional sequence involves two stages. In the first stage, it is necessary to take the performance objectives developed earlier and establish a meaningful sequence for accomplishing each objective. In the second stage, covered in the last part of this chapter, you will need to take each objective and develop a specific instructional strategy for accomplishing it.

Sequencing instruction is really just a process of identifying the natural relationships between objectives and of establishing a learning hierarchy based on those relationships.

To develop an instructional sequence, the first thing you should do is go back to your performance objectives and begin to group related objectives together. Gagné (1977) proposed what has become one of the most effective and useful ways to group related objectives. He found that complex behaviors and tasks are invariably composed of simpler behaviors and tasks, and that attainment of these behaviors is essential before the complex behavior can be learned. He suggested, therefore, that the most appropriate form of sequencing be based on a learning hierarchy that reflects this complex task-subtask relationship. The key question that needs to be asked in terms of this approach is, What

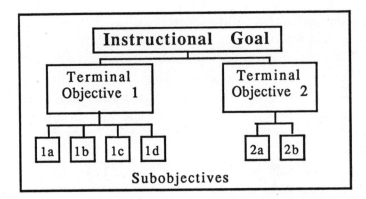

Figure 2.4   Sequencing a hierarchy of objectives

skill or knowledge does the learner need to have before he/she can perform the next higher task or behavior? If the answer is "none," then you are at the lowest level of the hierarchy. Any other response will begin the development of a learning hierarchy and a potential sequence for instruction.

Once you are satisfied that you have identified *all* of the performance objectives the learner must meet, and have grouped those performance objectives in a learning hierarchy, the next step is to arrange equal levels of objectives into a functional instructional sequence.

Figure 2.4 illustrates one way to define an instructional sequence. The hierarchy suggests a flexible instructional sequence. It doesn't matter what order the lower-level subobjectives (1a, b, c, & 2a, b) are performed in, as long as they are all met before the associated terminal or higher-level objective is attempted.

The illustrations shown in Figure 2.5 are referred to as learning

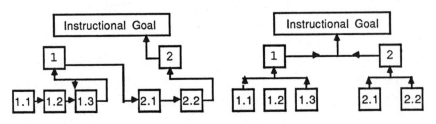

Figure 2.5   Learning maps

maps. Learning maps can be used to show both the hierarchy and sequence relationship that exists among different levels of objectives and goals. In a learning map, when boxes are connected by a line or arrow, the implication is that a direct, logical relationship exists between those objectives. Where the boxes are not connected, no such relationship exists. Boxes that appear higher on the map indicate higher levels of terminal objectives; i.e., objectives that require prerequisite objectives.

Look again at the left learning map shown in Figure 2.5. Applying the rules just described, we can see that there is a direct relationship between objectives 1.1, 1.2, and 1.3, but it is not a hierarchical relationship. What this means is that knowledge of how to perform objective 1.2 is not dependent on knowledge of how to perform objective 1.1. If the ability to perform one objective is prerequisite to the ability to perform another objective, the objectives must appear in a vertical relationship on the learning map. Such relationships are extremely important when it comes to designing the final computer program.

In deciding whether a direct relationship exists between various objectives, examine each objective. Determine what inputs (previous knowledge or skill) the objective requires, and what outcomes will result when the objective is mastered. If, in order for a learner to meet the stated objective, he/she must already have acquired a specific skill or concept, then the objective that has that skill or concept as its outcome or output becomes a prerequisite to the objective you are working with. The fact that a skill is used before another skill, in a job-related sense, does not necessarily mean that any direct relationship exists between the two skills, or that learning one skill is necessarily prerequisite to learning another skill which is used later on the job.

When you have finished developing the learning map for your objectives, double check it for:

- *Unnecessary objectives*—objectives that are nice to know, or to be able to do, but that fail to add anything to any terminal objective or the program's overall instructional goal.

- *Incorrectly positioned objectives*—objectives that have been incorrectly positioned according to sequence or hierarchy.
- *Unlisted objectives*—prerequisite or terminal objectives that are essential to meeting the overall instructional goal.

When designing lessons for computer based application, it is recommended that no lesson or lesson module take longer than 15 to 20 minutes to complete. This time limit is recommended, among other things, so that learners can come and go from the courseware at natural breaking points. From your learning map you should be able to identify groups of related objectives that could be met within the 15- to 20-minute time frame. These groups become the building blocks for the major segments of your program.

There are many ways to look at relationships between objectives. The final instructional sequences could, for example, be based on the learning hierarchy just developed, or on a learner's interests, familiar to unfamiliar tasks, general to specific tasks, concrete to abstract concepts, content or presentation similarities, subject matter considerations, or a chronological sequence based on use or job performance. As you identify relationships between objectives, take some, if not all, of these approaches into account.

Thus far, the control over both sequencing and hierarchy has been based on a direct relationship being established between each of the various parts. But what criteria do you use for sequencing if no direct relationship exists between certain parts? The following recommendations may help you sequence objectives and the related instruction when prerequisite guidelines don't exist:

Let the learner decide.   Whenever possible, let the learner determine the sequence. It may be necessary to force a learner to complete all of one group of objectives before going on to the next group. But, if it doesn't matter in which order a particular objective is met, inform the learner what the objectives are and let them choose the one that appears most relevant or interesting.

Group according to related content. While the objectives may not be directly related, similarities and overlaps in content or instructional approach may exist between certain objectives. Grouping instruction according to such similarities may make learning more efficient and effective for the learner, and it may make programming the lesson easier by eliminating the duplication of subroutines and/or graphics used in teaching both objectives.

Concrete to abstract. Concrete concepts and skills are usually learned easier and more quickly than concepts and skills that are more abstract or that have less direct application to the real world. If those objectives having direct application are taught first, it is more likely that the learner will discover an application for those that come after.

Motivating to less motivating. While it would be nice to believe that all learning is equally motivating, the fact is that it is not. A lesson or lesson segment should begin with the most motivating objective possible. As the lesson progresses, mix the motivating and less motivating segments so that the learner doesn't reach a point where all the fun is gone and just the work is left.

Familiar to unfamiliar. Learning occurs best when it can be attached or associated with something the learner already knows, feels a need for, or has an interest in. Instruction should generally start with something known and move through logical steps deeper into the unknown.

2.4   SPECIFYING ENTRY BEHAVIOR

In the process of analyzing the tasks and concepts you want to teach with your program, you have hopefully listed some skills and/or concepts that your audience already possesses. If your target audience includes more than a few people, you can expect at least some exceptions to the analysis descriptions you have developed. Accepting these limitations, your next step is to define an entry level and specific entry behaviors which will guide the development of your courseware package.

Entry behaviors are really just learning objectives which, based on the audience analysis, you assume each of the members of your target audience has already mastered. Some entry behaviors are generally applicable to almost any learning experience. Reading level, attention span, motivation, problem-solving ability are all examples of entry behaviors that affect the outcome of learning but are not content specific. Things like grade in school, sex, and race are rarely, if ever, significant entry behaviors since, within these categories, are found almost every possible level of entry performance.

Some entry behaviors are a direct part of the tasks and skills that will make up the selected content area. To determine these entry behaviors, you need to compare what you have learned from your instructional analysis with what you know about your target audience. If you go far enough in your instructional analysis, you should discover the cut off point at which the majority of your audience are already capable of performing the tasks and skills you have defined. Everything beyond that point defines the tasks and skills the target audience needs to be taught. Everything behind or below that point are entry behaviors that you probably can assume can be performed by the target audience when they start the courseware package.

The selection of the cut-off point is critical. If you set the point too high, your courseware will probably not succeed with a large percentage of the target audience. If you select a point too low, many of your targeted learners will get bored and quit the program before reaching the skills they need to learn. If you are unsure or can't locate an appropriate point, go back to your instructional and audience analyses and continue working with these analyses until you are sure that an appropriate entry point can be established.

Entry behaviors should be specific, and there should be some way of evaluating whether they have been met or not. The criteria for writing a good entry behavior specification is the same criteria used in writing effective learning objectives.

* Specify the skill, task, or behavior which the learner will be expected to perform.
* Establish the criteria that will be used to evaluate whether the learner has achieved the desired result.

The following are examples of entry behavior statements:

The learner should be able to load and operate an Apple computer without any outside help.

The learner should be able to define and use active voice, positive form, and concrete language in writing newspaper articles.

The learner should be able to read at a fifth-grade level.

2.5   INSTRUCTIONAL STRATEGIES

Previous stages in the planning process provided you with an understanding of **WHY** the program you are designing is needed and **WHAT** the content of the program should deal with or help accomplish. You also should have developed some guidelines which you can use to determine **WHEN** a particular objective should be taught or presented. The next question that needs to be answered is **HOW?** Determining the best strategy to use in teaching an instructional goal, and how a particular objective should be achieved or presented, is not always an easy question to answer. Before attempting to give guidelines on designing individual computer frames to meet specific objectives, you need to make some decisions that affect the design of your entire program.

Saying that you are going to use interactive computer based instruction as the strategy for presenting or accomplishing an instructional goal is just slightly less general than saying that you are going to use media to present that goal. Interactive CBI is a general term that gets applied to an extremely broad group of instructional strategies. About the only thing that some of these strategies have in common is the fact that the computer presents some, and manages all, of the resources provided to the learner. As computer systems, and devices such as videodisc and compact disc (C.D.) players, which can be controlled by the computer, become less expensive and more powerful, it is likely that CBI will become even more of a combined media strategy.

Choosing the right strategy

The first thing you need to decide is what CBI strategy is appropriate and will be most effective in helping the learner meet the program's objectives.

Most CBI strategies can be classified into one or more of the categories shown in Figure 2.6.

To help you determine which, if any, of these strategies you should use, let's take a closer look at some of the advantages and disadvantages, and design criteria associated with each.

Tutorials

A tutorial strategy is intended to emulate the "ideal" teaching situation of one learner with one or more teachers. Unfortunately, many designers have interpreted this to mean that the computer carries out a limited question-and-answer dialogue with the person sitting at the computer terminal. Many tutorials are really just computer based versions of the linear programmed text approach. A learner is presented with a small amount of information, which

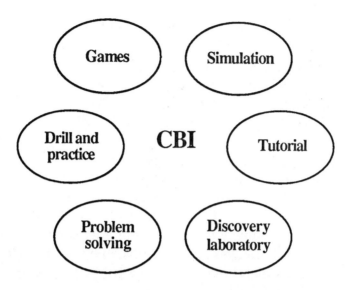

Figure 2.6   Computer based instructional strategies

is followed by a question that checks to see if the learner understood the information. If they did, the program proceeds. If they didn't, the program redisplays the missed concept. Such an approach fails to make use of the power and some of the unique qualities of modern computer systems.

The "ideal" teaching environment includes more than just a teacher and student; it includes a vast number of resources including films, books, worksheets, pictures, and so on. In that ideal environment the teacher would not only conduct a dialogue with the learner but also:

- *Individualize presentations*, taking into account the learner's background and entry behaviors, and provide supplemental or remedial instruction which is responsive to a particular problem a learner may be having.
- *Generate questions and present problems*, which did more than test the learner's ability to memorize, and which provide practice in areas where the learner is weak, rather than continually reevaluating the learner's strengths.
- *Provide outside resources*, where appropriate, including audio and visual materials.

- *Require the learner to be present only until a concept or objective has been mastered.*
- *Keep accurate records of student progress*, and use the information to control and modify the instructional approach.
- *Provide instruction at a rate suitable to the learner's ability.*
- *Permit the learner to decide when he/she is ready to be tested on a concept or objective.*
- *Encourage experimentation* by providing both the problem to solve and the resources needed to solve the problem, and do everything possible to assure that learning occurred.

While there are many things the computer can't provide the learner, most of the above could be provided by a computer based tutorial with a little effort and creativity on your part as the developer.

Drill-and-practice

The drill-and-practice strategy is most appropriately used when learners are already familiar with the rules associated with a concept, skill, or system, and where learning can best be promoted by allowing them to try out the rules with additional problems or practice.

Generally the drill-and-practice strategy has been applied where memorization is the main vehicle for learning; i.e., spelling, math tables, vocabulary problems, and so on. It is especially effective in instruction requiring paired association between two or more pieces of information. Foreign language translation, music sight/sound drill, and cause–effect relationships can all effectively be taught using a drill-and-practice strategy.

If a drill-and-practice strategy is to be effective it should meet most of the following characteristics:

- Feedback should be provided on a regular basis throughout the drill-and-practice experience.
- Alternate and increasingly more difficult levels of drill and practice should be provided.

- Problems should be randomly generated or randomly ordered so that the problem can be used more than once by the same user without just repeating the same exact sequence of problems.
- Problems should challenge the learner's ability and should get increasingly more difficult as the learner demonstrates an ability to solve easier problems.
- A variable entry level option should be provided so that learners and/or teachers can assign appropriate problem levels.
- A record-keeping and reporting system should be provided so that learners can receive appropriate feedback and can compare results from one practice session to the next.

Simulations

The simulation strategy has as its basis a computer model that represents a scientific or social event or phenomenon. In a simulation, learners are allowed to manipulate simplified situations that are analogous to the real situation. Use of a simulation strategy is most appropriate when the information or skill being taught has a direct application in the real world, and where one aspect of the learning goal is to prepare people to better understand and/or control a portion of reality.

In determining whether the simulation strategy is appropriate to your program, one of the first things you should consider is whether an appropriate model of the real world can be described in ways that the computer can utilize and from which the learner can discover a valid relationship. Before the computer can operate a simulation model, the model must be described in mathematical and/or logical terms. Almost anyone can set up and sell lemonade at a neighborhood stand, but describing the interaction that takes place between the weather, traffic conditions, prices of sugar, advertising, etc., and to express that interaction *accurately* in the form of a mathematical and/or logical model, is an entirely different problem.

To be effective and accurate, most CBI models should be based on some research of statistics. If a simulation strategy is adopted, teachers and learners should be provided the background of the model so they can judge its accuracy and do their part to refine or build new and more useful models.

Simulations, in addition to coming up with an accurate mathematical or logical way of describing the world, must also be able to select and define a finite portion of the environment within which to operate. Computer simulations cannot include all of the information and options available in the real world. If you choose to apply this strategy you will need to define the essential aspects that make up an accurate but simplified portion of reality.

The simulation strategy has been successfully applied in the acquisition of numerous job-related skills including: flight instruction and driving skills, machine operation, and scientific instrument interpretation. Most of the learning outcomes associated with these types of simulations are usually criterion-based, i.e., based on a preset standard of performance.

Simulations have also been used to help learners discover the nature of scientific, social, economic, or environmental systems. In these simulations, learners can be given the chance not only to learn the relevant facts about these systems, but to manipulate various system parameters to discover the cause-and-effect relationships that exist within a system. Simulations can be used to help learners internalize facts, feelings, and ideas, and are one of the most effective ways of achieving effective instructional objectives via the computer.

If the simulation strategy is selected you will need to:

- Identify the critical elements which make up the environment to be simulated.
- Quantify with a mathematical or logical formula each of the critical elements.
- Establish a context within which the simulation will occur. This includes a motivational as much as a factual context. The best simulations are those where some role playing is involved.
- Establish an entry point. Simulations can spend a great deal

of time setting up the situation. Learners must be provided current status and relevant facts very quickly.

- Identify methods of manipulation. Determine what the learner's role will be in the simulations and what and how the learner will be allowed to manipulate in the simulation model.
- Describe the learner/computer interactive model. Determine how the learner provided data and decisions will interact with the computer manipulated variables.
- Establish critical and alternative paths which the learner will be allowed to travel as a consequence of the decision-making process.
- Establish appropriate criteria for judging the effectiveness of the simulation experience.
- Provide the learner with a sense of involvement and competition, with success based on personal expertise and not just learning how to "beat the system."
- Establish a reward structure that provides the "thrill of victory and the agony of defeat." The reward structure should fit into and be a natural part of the simulation model, presenting as realistically as possible the reward structure that exists in the actual environment.

Problem solving

In many instructional situations the goal is not to teach facts but to develop a student's ability to formulate, analyze, and solve problems; or to encourage the extension of knowledge through either an inductive or a deductive process. Both of these situations call for an instructional strategy that is more flexible than those discussed above and that uses the computer as a tool to encourage and aid in the problem-solving process.

The learner's role in a problem-solving CBI strategy is to formulate the questions and strategies that will lead to an appropriate solution to a problem. The computer's role is to present the problem, to provide on request the relevant facts and resources required to solve the problem, to make sure the learner doesn't lose track of the problem, and to act as a tool for the learner.

The problem-solving strategy can be used, in conjunction with other strategies, to expand a learner's understanding beyond the specific information or examples provided in a lesson. The problem-solving strategy can be used to allow the learner to explore and discover more of the applications and ramifications surrounding the concepts and skills which they have been taught.

One useful variation of the problem-solving strategy encourages either inductive or deductive thinking to occur. In one strategy, learners are presented with a series of examples and nonexamples. The learner must, without specific prompts, identify and separate the examples from the nonexamples. In the process he/she is required to derive or infer a rule which must then be applied to other sets of examples and nonexamples. The goal of this strategy is to encourage a learner to develop general concepts and rules which can be applied to organizing the world around them.

The opposite approach could also be taken, where the learner is presented with a general rule or concept. The learner is then required to deduce new ways that the rule or concept may be applied in solving previously unrelated problems.

Discovery laboratory

The discovery laboratory strategy is by far the most unstructured of the CBI approaches. For many learners—especially the "gifted and talented," "non-academically inclined," and "instructionally handicapped"—and for many instructional goals, the best instructional strategy is an experience based or performance based learning experience.

A computer based discovery laboratory is really just a computer-supported simulation of the tools and experiences that make up the world around us, minus many of the risks that limit our experimenting with that environment. As an independent program, the strategy can best be used with a target audience of independent learners. This strategy can also be used by teachers to support and enhance their live instruction, encouraging nonindependent learners to become more independent.

The discovery laboratory is the environment in which discovery learning can occur. Learners are provided with the tools for analyzing, exploring, and testing out new concepts and skills.

The discovery lab "equipment" may be as "simple" as the turtle used in the discovery laboratory called LOGO, or it may be a very complex lab, allowing simulated or computer-controlled physics, chemistry, or even social experiments.

The computer, with its ability to be attached to numerous external devices and with its own internal capabilities, is a natural learning center where old concepts can be discovered and new knowledge generated.

Games

Games are considered by many to be an inappropriate use of computers in instruction; but, if properly and carefully designed, games can be an effective CBI strategy.

Generally, when we think of something as a "game," we do so because it's fun, motivating, and entertaining. Obviously not all games are instructional. Many games are played purely for entertainment, where "winning" is the result of chance rather than of any acquired skill.

Many games, though, have strict rules. When followed, they help the learner acquire highly sophisticated skills and concepts. For example, it is a common practice in the military to "play" what are called "war games," which are used to train and develop modern war skills and strategies. Ancient and modern scholars played games of strategy to develop their problem-solving skills. Sometimes the only difference between a game that is designed for entertainment and one that has educational application is the degree of accuracy of the rules to real-life situations, concepts, and systems.

Games are one of the most effective strategies for rewarding and motivating a learner. An instructional game can be included within a tutorial program as a reward for completing a certain number of units or learning a specified number of competencies.

If properly designed, instructional games are often difficult to distinguish from good simulations or drill-and-practice programs. Games in this context are really just fun, motivating, and entertaining CBI programs.

If you are going to use the game strategy for your CBI, you should carefully analyze your objectives for the basic concepts to be taught and tie the outcome of the game directly to the achievement of those concepts.

You will need to come up with a game vehicle and develop a set of rules to structure the game around. While it may be possible for you to come up with a totally original game, as a starting point it is recommended that you look at some of the more popular games on the market today for ideas. The game of Monopoly has, for example, been used as the basis on which to design many instructional games to teach everything from ecology to sportsmanship. Many of the popular arcade games can be modified to provide a vehicle for rapid-paced drill-and-practice of math and word skills. Being able to give a correct response in order to blow the alien spaceship out of the sky is a lot more fun than simply being asked a question, giving a response, and being told that you got the answer "correct" or "incorrect."

If a game is to be instructional, it must meet the following criteria:

- *It must be based on constructs that accurately represent and reflect the concept or skill being taught.*
- *Success must be a result of the learner's ability to master the concept, skill, and constructs upon which the game was based.*
- *The learner must be aware of the concepts or skills that are to be mastered and not perceive that they are just learning to "play a game."*

Describing the strategy

The purpose for developing a strategy is to facilitate and ensure that learning takes place. A description of the learning strategy provides the framework around which your program will be developed. It also will be used at the end of the development process as a comparison document when you evaluate your program, to see whether you accomplished what you set out to accomplish. Even if you are going to do all the program development yourself, it is important for you to write down a specific description of the strategies you are going to use. Six elements are important:

1.   *Program's goals and objectives.*   List the program's instructional goal and all the performance objectives you have established which will be met by the particular program you are working on.

2.   *Program treatment.*   Provide a general description of the treatment you plan to use. If, for example, you decide that a drill-and-practice approach is the best way to facilitate the accomplishment of your objectives, what type of drill-and-practice do you plan to use; i.e., what general procedures will be followed in presenting a stimulus and receiving a response. You should describe, in a general way, each major event that will occur as the program develops.

3.   *Modular development.*   The third part of the strategy describes the size of the instructional "chunks," or events, and the amount of time and program space to be allocated for each module. You need to indicate how much of the total instructional time you plan to allow for each of the major events in your program and what percent of your program will be allocated to meeting each of your intended objectives. And you should anticipate approximately how much of the learner's time it should take to complete each of the intended sublessons. It is important to establish these parameters early. Experience has shown that, as you begin to develop the actual program, each module rapidly begins to grow into a self-contained program. Allocate a reasonable amount of time, and program space to accomplish an objective; and then stick to it.

4.   *Interactive strategies.*   The strategy should include the practice, feedback, and interactive techniques that will be used in the

program. Match as closely as possible the interaction requirements of the program with the performance criteria the learner will be required to meet under the guidelines established in the related instructional objective. That is, if the learner is going to be expected to play a musical piece to demonstrate proficiency on a given objective, then the interactive strategy should at least provide the learner with the opportunity to play a similar musical piece. If the learner is to identify certain cause-and-effect relationships, then the interactive strategies should include similar identifying requirements.

Besides having interactive strategies directly related to demonstrating proficiency on specified objectives, interactive strategies should be related as closely as possible to real-life applications.

5. *Remediation and enrichment strategies.* A description of the remediation and enrichment strategies you believe are essential to include in your program should be included in the strategy document. This section should cause you to look at the target audience and your proposed content more carefully. You should attempt to identify and anticipate areas in the program where it is likely that the learner will have major problems, and your instructional strategy should prescribe options which will handle these problem areas. If your program is going to provide any enrichment options; i.e., options that allow the fast learner to go beyond the normal portion of the program, then these options should be described in this section as well.

6. *Content outline, script, or flow chart.* A specific content outline, script, or flow chart should be included as the final portion of the specification document. As you develop the content outline, continually look back at your established objectives to make sure you include all of the necessary content but not that content which has nothing to do with meeting the established objectives.

As you can see, the strategy document pulls together all of the major elements that will make up your program. If done properly, the strategy document will guide the actual development of the final computer program and will provide you with a benchmark that you can use to test the success or failure of your courseware package when it is completed.

2.6 SUMMARY

Instructional analysis is a process used to identify and sequence the essential skill, knowledge, and attitudes required to achieve an instructional goal in the most efficient and effective way possible.

The analysis should examine the job performance skill required, the input and output requirements of the goal, and the intellectual behaviors involved. Before an instructional analysis can be considered finished, it should be:

- *Complete*—all steps necessary to perform the task or goal are present.
- *Finite*—each task and subtask defines a specific beginning and ending point.
- *Unambiguous*—each subtask can be read and interpreted in only one way.
- *Operational*—each subtask tells specifically what the learner needs to do or know in order to complete the subtask.

For each subtask that is identified, one or more specific performance objectives should be written. Each objective should contain a statement of the:

- Behavior—skill or task to be performed.
- Condition—environment which will prevail when the task is performed.
- Standard—criteria used to evaluate the learner's performance.

In addition, all performance objectives should be written from the learner's point of view and be measurable.

Objectives are grouped and sequenced according to a learning/performance hierarchy. A learning map is used to describe the hierarchy and sequence relationships between different levels of objectives and goals.

Entry behaviors are established by comparing the learner's present skills and knowledge, as assessed through an audience analysis, and the desired skills and knowledge, as determined in the instructional analysis. The entry level should be set to the general capabilities of the average user. Specific statements of entry behaviors should be written following the same guidelines established for writing performance objectives.

Developing an instructional strategy begins with the selection of a basic CBI strategy. The decision should be based on the instructional goal and performance criteria which have been established.

CBI strategies generally fall into six categories: tutorial, drill-and-practice, simulation, problem solving, discovery laboratory, and games. Each strategy has its own set of advantages, disadvantages, and design requirements, which should be taken into consideration in selecting the strategy most appropriate for a given instructional goal.

Decisions involving the instructional strategy should be documented. The document should include:

1. A listing of the program's performance goals and objectives.
2. A description of the treatment to be applied.
3. A description of the individual modules and events that will make up the courseware package.
4. A description of the interactive strategies that will be applied.
5. Remediation and enrichment strategies and options which will be included in the package.
6. A sequenced content/management outline, script, and/or

flowchart that describes precisely the events, decisions, and content that will be included in the program.

2.7 ISSUES AND ACTIVITIES

1. Identify an instructional goal to work with and decide which form of instructional analysis will yield the most accurate information on related subtasks.
2. Take a chapter from a textbook and write performance objectives which you feel describe the major behaviors being taught by the chapter. Compare your objectives with those of another student who worked independently on the same chapter.
3. Observe an expert in some area doing a specific task. Write down all the things you observe and then see if you can replicate the task with only the information contained in your notes. If you have problems, see if you can discover what elements you failed to observe or record.
4. Identify the relevant entry behaviors for a fifth-grade math class. Test a group of entering fifth-graders to determine how many of them meet the behaviors you anticipated.
5. Identify what you believe are the performance objectives for this chapter and perform an analysis using Bloom's taxonomy to determine what level of cognitive achievement is being taught.
6. Review a collection of courseware packages and decide which CBI strategy or strategies would best describe the general nature of the program.
7. List all of the performance criteria associated with a learning objective. Next to each criteria list some ways the computer could be used to test whether that criteria has been met.
8. Using the lists described above, make a list of the decisions

the computer would have to make and the criteria it could use to make each decision. Make sure every possible choice or option is covered.

9. Design an instructional strategy to achieve five instructional objectives. Play the role of the computer and try out your strategy on a small group of learners.

10. Using an instructional goal identified earlier, prepare a complete strategy document.

11. Using a commercial courseware package, analyze it for the strategy information outlined in this chapter. Prepare a document that describes the strategy that was used.

2.8 REFERENCES

Bloom, B. S. *Taxonomy of Educational Objectives, Handbook 1: Cognitive Domain*. New York: McKay, 1956.

Bloom, B. S. *Human Characteristics and School Learning*. New York: McGraw-Hill, 1976.

Briggs, L. J. (ed.). *Instructional Design: Principles and Applications*. Englewood Cliffs, NJ: Educational Technology Publications, 1981.

Briggs, L. J., & Wager, W. W. *Handbook of Procedures for the Design of Instruction* (2nd ed.). Englewood Cliffs, NJ: Educational Technology Publications, 1981.

Burke, R. L. *CAI Sourcebook*. Englewood Cliffs, NJ: Prentice-Hall, 1982.

Carlisle, K. E. *Analyzing Jobs and Tasks*. Englewood Cliffs, NJ: Educational Technology Publications, 1986.

Davies, I. K. *The Organization of Training*. New York: McGraw-Hill, 1973.

Davies, I. K. *Competency Based Learning*. New York: McGraw-Hill, 1973.

Davies, I. K. *Objectives in Curriculum Design*. London: McGraw-Hill, 1976.

Davies, I. K. *Instructional Technique*. New York: McGraw-Hill, 1981.

Davis, R. H., Alexander, L. T., & Yelon, S. L. *Learning System Design*. New York: McGraw-Hill, 1975.

DeCecco, J. P. *The Psychology of Learning and Instruction: Educational Psychology*. Englewood Cliffs, NJ: Prentice-Hall, 1968.

Dick, W., & Carey, L. *The Systematic Design of Instruction* (2nd ed.). Glenview, IL: Scott, Foresman & Co., 1985.

Gagné, R. M. *Conditions of Learning* (3rd ed.). New York: Holt, Rinehart & Winston, 1977.

Gagné, R. M., & Briggs, L. J. *Principles of Instructional Design* (2nd ed.). New York: Holt, Rinehart & Winston, 1978.

Hannum, W. H. Task analysis procedures. *NSPI Journal, 19*(3)(1980):16–17.

Hofmeister, A. *Microcomputer Applications in the Classroom.* New York: Holt, Rinehart & Winston, 1984.

Journal of Instructional Development, 6(4)(1983).

Kaufman, R. A. *Educational System Planning.* Englewood Cliffs, NJ: Prentice-Hall, 1972.

Kibler, R. J., Cegala, D. J., et al. *Objectives for Instruction and Evaluation.* Boston: Allyn & Bacon, 1974.

Mager, R. F. *Preparing Instructional Objectives.* Palo Alto, CA: Fearon Publishers, 1975.

Merrill, P. F. Representations for algorithms. *NSPI Journal, 19*(2)(1980):11–15.

Roberts, W. K. Preparing instructional objectives: Usefulness revisited. *Educational Technology, 22*(7)(1982):15–19.

Taylor, R. P. (ed.). *The Computer in the School: Tutor, Tool, Tutee.* New York: Teachers College Press, 1980.

3

The Management of Instruction

3.0 INTRODUCTION

Chapters 1 and 2 dealt with the content, instructional sequence, and strategy of an interactive computer based instructional program. To be effective, a program needs one additional major design component. This component, the management of the delivery system, is generally translated into five major functions:

- *Assessment*—collecting individual performance information and system performance information.
- *Diagnosis*—the ongoing process of determining learner needs.
- *Learning prescription*—matching the needs of the individual learner with the appropriate amount and type of instruction.
- *Record keeping*—maintaining a record of performance and other critical data for use in future diagnosis and prescription.
- *Reporting*—providing meaningful reports of performance for both the teacher and the learner.

It should be obvious that, if all of the above are complete and in sufficient detail, the management portion of your program could require that you design a program much larger and more difficult than the instructional program itself. That is why you will see management packages specifically designed to perform the five functions listed above and nothing else. It is not the purpose of this chapter to teach you how to design a large, stand-alone management system but rather, to suggest some management functions that can—and should—be built into many of the interactive programs you develop.

A major goal of interactive computer based courseware has always been to emulate as closely as possible the one-teacher, one-learner instructional environment. In that ideal environment, as in the traditional classroom, the teacher not only delivers the instruction but is also responsible for managing the delivery process, collecting the data, and evaluating both the student's performance and the performance of the instructional process. All of the information collected is then used by the teacher to control future instructional decisions. This same procedure is the goal of management, as it relates to interactive learning packages. Courseware should at least include a management component that guides the delivery system toward achieving the most effective and efficient instructional process possible and that makes both the learner and delivery system accountable for their performance.

You may not be able to include all of the management components discussed here in your CBI package; but you should make every effort to help the teacher and the learner carry out these functions in other ways. Providing an on-line, or external, management component with your courseware package helps legitimize it. Doing this allows your package to meet two criteria that are basic to effective instructional systems; i.e., accountability and systematic improvement. Learners, teachers, and your program must all be held accountable for meeting intended objectives. As an instructional designer, always look for ways to systematically improve the effectiveness of the instructional process. A management component, if properly designed, will provide the information your program needs to carry out both of these important functions.

3.1 ASSESSMENT

The management of the learning process begins with the assessment of individual performance. Unfortunately, the tendency is to equate assessment with testing. But testing is just one of the tools available to help you and the computer assess the current status of the learner. In interacting with a learner, a teacher observes, among other things, how quickly and how confidently the learner answers the question and whether the learner is able to generalize and justify the response. A computer can't analyze a learner's body language, but it can take into account many of the same criteria teachers use to assess learner needs and abilities.

In designing an assessment system, specific decisions must be made in order to deliver the most efficient and effective amount of information or practice. The major purpose of any assessment system should be to allow the computer, learner, and/or teacher to draw a conclusion and/or make a decision. The data, or information, collected during the assessment process, and the instruments used to collect that data, should relate directly to those decisions.

Computer based assessment systems can be designed to collect information in three categories: affective, cognitive, and psychomotor.

Affective refers to the attitudes a learner brings to, or takes away from, an instructional experience. Some computer based instructional programs, especially simulations, are designed more to change attitudes than to provide the learner with new information. Attitudes affect the motivation of the learner, the ability of a learner to interpret information, and many other aspects of the learning process. Being able to assess and make decisions about attitudes is very important to many instructional programs.

Cognitive refers to learners' skills in thinking, learning, and remembering information and ideas, not just to some facts memorized and reported back. Too often the assessment of cognitive skills is really just a test of a learner's ability to communicate verbally. For example, multiple choice questions only test whether or not a learner has recognized the proper verbal description of a concept. But if the concept is abstract, e.g., the theory of relativity, a verbal description of it is probably inadequate and verbal assessment therefore unfair. Designers of computer based instructional management modules need to find nonverbal assessment tools to complement the traditional verbal ones—if cognitive assessment is to be successful and accurate.

The third category is psychomotor, or motor, skills. I prefer the term "psychomotor" because it recognizes the interrelationship between the brain and the muscles. Understanding this relationship is an important part of assessing a learner's ability to perform. For example, the physical ability to write a letter of the alphabet on a piece of paper may be directly related to the ability of the brain to form the correct image of the letter. For years teachers have watched students form letters and other visual images backwards, or in what appeared to be a very confused manner. They assumed that the child just could not write. Today we understand more about dyslexia, recognizing it to be as much of a cognitive as a muscle impairment. Psychomotor assessment should include the cognitive aspect, not just the outward muscular expression of behavior.

Designing an assessment system

Designing a computer based instruction assessment system is a four-stage process. First, decide on the type of decisions and conclusions that the computer, the teacher, and/or the learner will have to make. Second, determine the appropriate data/information for making the best possible decision. Third, select an instrument or strategy that will permit the computer to collect the essential data. And fourth, establish the rules that will govern the decision outcome, i.e., IF this situation exists THEN this will be the decision or conclusion. Figure 3.1 shows the four stages as they might appear on a single design worksheet.

DECISION:
   Can the learner recognize an Iambic poetic rhythm pattern
   from a Dactylic rhythmic pattern with 90% accuracy?

RELEVANT DATA:
   Learners recognition response to 10 Iambic and Dactylic
   rhythmic patterns.

INSTRUMENT:
   Multiple-choice criterion frame containing 10 Iambic and 6 Dactylic
   patterns. Learners will be required to select all Iambic patterns
   from the set.

RULE:
   IF 9 out of 10 Iambic patterns are selected THEN move to next lesson
       ELSE - repeat lesson
   IF 1 Dactylic pattern is selected THEN give learner option to repeat
   IF>1 Dactylic pattern is selected THEN repeat lesson

Figure 3.1   Assessment design worksheet

Decisions and conclusions

Decisions required by a particular program may be absolute or relative. Absolute decisions are generally criterion based, having only two choices, e.g., right or wrong, go or don't go, pass or fail. Relative decisions are made by comparing two or more related pieces of information. In many simulations there is no absolute right or wrong way to solve the problem. In games such as Monopoly and chess, outcomes are never determined by the right or wrong choice of a single move but on the relative moves that each learner takes in succession. It's important to understand the type of decision required if appropriate data are to be collected and analyzed.

When preparing your list of decisions, consider those that affect the following.

Learner performance. The most important reason for having a management component in your program is to help the computer decide how the learner is performing and what the best instructional strategy is to match that performance. Some decisions to consider are:

- What prerequisite skills does the learner lack?
- Is the learner meeting the established criteria for acceptable performance?
- Do the learner's decisions lead to a logical solution?
- Is the rate at which the learner is responding acceptable?
- Has the learner's performance on this practice session improved over that of previous practice sessions?

Learning sequence. One of the goals of computer based instruction is to individualize the sequence and rate of presentation to meet the needs of the individual learner. To meet this goal, some decisions to be made are:

- What is the best learning track for this student?
- Is the rate of presentation appropriate? If not, how should it be changed?
- What is the next recommended lesson segment?
- Does the learner need to repeat the question?
- How many times has the learner repeated the question or lesson segment?

Learning activities. Individualization also implies that not all learners need the same instructional activities at the same time. Determining when remediation or additional practice is needed should be one of the functions of the management component of your program. Some of the learning activity-related questions that your program design might include are:

- Which activity does the learner need or wish to participate in?

- Does the learner need more information or more practice?
- Does the learner wish to repeat the most recent activity?
- What remedial activities are needed by this learner?

Course management. Keeping track of the learner is necessary, whether the instruction is being presented by a live teacher or by a series of computer based instructional lessons. Teachers and learners need to know what they have worked on, what they need to work on, and how they did. If a learner is permitted to stop in the middle of a lesson, then additional management decisions must be made to prevent wasting time repeating information. Some decisions that may be required by your program are:

- Which lessons has the learner started and/or completed?
- What is the learner's final score/grade on this lesson?
- On what date and at what time did the learner take this lesson?
- How many times did it take the learner to complete this lesson?
- What is the learner's current location in the lesson?
- Does the learner need to leave a message for the instructor?

Collecting the right data

You have now determined the kinds of decisions that will be required and who or what will make them. Next, you need to determine what data or information the computer has to collect and what techniques or instruments will allow you to collect it.

Assessment data is the information your program collects for use in making management decisions. It, like the corresponding decision types, can be classified into two categories. Criterion-referenced data is information that can be compared to a previously established standard. Computers are especially adept at collecting and using this type of data because it matches the logic structure of the computer itself. It is easy for a computer to compare a learner's response with a preprogrammed correct choice. It is more difficult for a computer to make such comparisons when any of the choices may be correct depending upon certain previous information. The fact that it is easier for the computer in the first instance does not mean that it is better, from a learning point of view. Criterion-referenced data and questions should only be used when the final decision serves an absolute function in the real environment.

Norm-referenced data is used to make relative decisions and conclusions. Input on a person's age may be judged as accurate or inaccurate, but if you want to know whether or not a person is overweight, age is just one of many factors in what must be considered a relative conclusion. Determining how to pay off a mortgage is a relative decision. It depends on the size of payments an individual can afford to make, the size of the down payment, the desired length of the payoff period, and so on. Generally, there is no absolute standard for reading speed. An individual's reading speed *and* comprehension must both be considered before an ideal reading speed can be determined for that individual. A decision on a learner's reading speed performance is relative to the learner's reading comprehension at that speed.

In most management decisions there are elements of criterion based decisions and normative/relative based decisions. In setting up an assessment system it is important to recognize and collect appropriate types of data and to use the appropriate data to make valid, accurate and reliable decisions.

What kind of information can the computer collect? Computers do, as you recognize, have some limits on the kind of information they can collect and analyze, but in most cases it is not the computer that limits the possibilities but the program designer. The following are just some of the many types of management data that can be collected and stored by a computer.

Actual responses.   This includes responses typed in through a keyboard as well as responses indicated through other peripheral devices, such as a light pen, touch sensitive screen, equipment simulators, and so on. Depending on how it will be used, data may be stored as the actual alphabetic or numerical input from the keyboard, as binary data, i.e., correct-incorrect, true-false, 1–0, etc., as screen coordinates, or as coded input values.

Competency standards. Data could indicate which competencies the learner has met and provide information on how close they came to those competencies the learner has not met.

Cumulative scores. Sometimes summary data is more useful in making decisions than the response or score on an individual item. Cumulative scores are useful for showing major trends, but they should not be grouped in such large chunks as to lose their impact on individual decisions. To be most effective, cumulative scores should be separated according to individual objectives and decisions, i.e., out of the 15 items on the post-test, which items related to objective #1, 2, etc., and of the five items the learner missed, which objective do they relate to. The number of items possible should be stored along with any cumulative score information.

Time/rate data. Many computers have a built-in clock or timing device which can provide critical data on such things as: response latency, i.e., the amount of time a learner spends on an individual item; time spent on an individual lesson or module; and the date(s) and time(s) when the learner was actually using the program.

Prescription data. If the computer is involved in prescribing the activities and sequence of instruction for an individual learner, then it is useful to have the computer maintain a learning map that shows or lists the sequence and activities the learner participated in.

Individualized assessment items. If the computer generates assessment items, or randomly assembles an assessment instrument from a pool of items, it is useful to maintain a record of the items each individual learner received.

Name of lessons and lesson segments started or completed. This information may be as general as the lesson name or as detailed as the individual frames which have been completed. The learner's current location in the lesson may be stored on the program disk and used to prescribe starting and stopping points each time the program is used by that learner.

Learner notes. These may be messages, response justifications, or comments left for a teacher's review; or they may be notes left by learners as reminders or for future reference when learner based decisions are made.

Repetitive data. This is how many times a learner has repeated a particular lesson, lesson segment, assessment item, or remedial sequence.

When determining the kinds of data the computer is going to collect, don't collect any data that is not going to be used by the learner, teacher, or computer in a decision-making process.

Delivery systems

Designing an assessment delivery system requires careful planning and an understanding of the purpose and function of the total computer based instructional package. One of the most important things to do is to establish unity among all instruction and management functions. The assessment process should not appear to the user as a separate part of your program, but as a natural result of the learning process. The management functions should provide the learner with frequent feedback on the progress they are making toward meeting the instructional objectives. Notice that I said "providing the *LEARNER* with frequent feedback." Many people involved in designing assessment systems forget that it is the learner, and the improvement of the learning process, that assessment is really about. The fact that a certain student missed 4 out of 9 questions is of little help to anyone. Assessment delivery systems should be designed to be responsive first to learner and learning needs, and second to teacher and other administrative needs.

Assessment may be one of the first things your program does. Designing a *SHORT* preassessment procedure may provide the computer with enough critical data to determine whether the learner has the prerequisite skills to gain from participating in the program. If the learner lacks these prerequisite skills, the program should suggest some outside resources where the learner might pick them up before beginning the courseware package.

Preassessment is useful in assigning learners a starting point in the program. In a multiplication drill and practice, for example, preassessment might be used to tell the computer what level of difficulty to use in generating the next problem. In a tutorial, it could be used to allow the computer or learner to skip previously learned materials. In a problem-solving interactive computer lesson, it could be used to establish some problem parameters— making the problem more relevant to the learner's needs.

When preassessment procedures are used they should be kept short, and they should appear relevant to the main function of the program. Learners may never reach the instructional portion of your program if the preassessment is too discouraging. If a learner misses every question on a preassessment, don't force the individual to suffer through it, even if it is just a preassessment. Preassessment questions should build on one another. If a learner can't respond correctly to a lower level question, obviously he or she won't be able to respond correctly to a higher level question that requires the use of the lower level information. Stop the assessment process when the computer has collected enough information to make a reasonably accurate decision. Don't continue to ask questions just because more questions are programmed into the computer.

During instruction, assessment should be interwoven with instructional materials to provide for short learning stages. Students should not have to wait until the end of a lesson to learn that they failed to understand something presented on the second or third frame of the program. As a general rule, no more than

10 to 15 frames should be presented to the learner without at least some form of assessment occurring.

Assessment should occur often enough so that approximately 80 percent or more of the responses given by a normal learner will be correct. Computer based instruction programs should not be designed to see how many learners can fail. Assessment should be used only as a tool to identify and prevent failure at the earliest possible point. Don't test until learners have a reasonable chance of passing. If problems can be identified early, it can save a lot of time and trouble correcting the problem. Even if no problem is found, the frequent positive feedback of assessment is the best motivator a designer can provide.

Almost every interaction should be considered a part of the assessment procedure. This may even include such a simple procedure as having the learner press the space bar to continue to the next frame. You may be asking "What kind of data can I get from a space bar?" Think for a moment about the kind of data you could get from watching a learner read a book. If the learner is just flipping through the pages at a rate too fast for reading, you might assume that the learner either can't understand the information and has given up or is searching for a particular piece of information. Most computer systems can provide information on how long a particular frame has been on the screen without a response from the learner. By checking this information, an assessment system may be able to identify a problem or need long before an actual testing frame is encountered. Response time may also be critical to a drill-and-practice program assessment. It is not unusual to find situations where learners don't know the right answer and also don't know how to proceed without giving an answer. Almost every response should have a maximum wait time associated with it, and when that is passed the assessment/management system should enter the process to determine the cause for the problem and prescribe an appropriate solution.

Numerous instruments and strategies have been developed and utilized in assessing learning performance. Observation of on-the-job performance, attitude questionnaires, and pencil-and-paper tests have been effective in assessing many aspects of learning. Each approach has its counterpart on the computer.

The observation of on-the-job performance. This is often approached through a computer based instruction simulation. On small computer systems, assessment of on-the-job performance is usually limited to assessing the decision-making ability of an individual in a simulated job environment. Flight simulators, i.e., computers that use simulated airplane controls as the input devices, have been used successfully for years in training and assessing pilots, not only in the decision-making and cognitive skills used in flying a plane, but in the affective and psychomotor skills as well. Such assessment tools have not generally been available on small computers, because program designers have been so tied in to the keyboard as the only input device. We must recognize that the keyboard is just one of many input devices a computer can understand. Once we do this we can increase the ability of the computer to assess and teach on-the-job performance based skills.

Attitude questionnaires. Computer generated and scored attitude questionnaires are often more accurate than those conducted by personal interview. Individuals are often willing to share feelings with a computer that they wouldn't reveal to any individual. Attitude data, while not providing a total assessment of the affective area, can be combined with other assessment data to help make important decisions.

Pencil-and-paper tests. The computer is a master of the pencil-and-paper test. Not only is it capable of giving a test that looks almost identical to the standard paper test, but also it can randomly generate the items and even some of the questions it includes on the test, individualizing each test for each learner. Sometimes the ease with which a computer can create paper-type tests results in their overuse in the assessment process. Designers of computer based instructional programs often turn to computer generated "paper" tests, when they should be using other assessment capabilities available on the computer. It's not that pen-cil-and-paper tests are bad, even when they are computer generated, it's just that most never get beyond the lowest level of the cognitive process, i.e., the ability to name, list, identify, recall, and so on. While useful at some levels, instructional as-sessment should deal with more than just the ability of the learner to recall unrelated facts. The three types of instruments discussed here are by no means the only ones that can be used to assess learner performance.

Item construction

As you design the instruments and questions to be used by the computer to collect learner performance data, follow these few simple guidelines.

Use valid assessment techniques and questions. Validity requires that the techniques and questions used to collect the data should be directly related to the content being sought. In addition to being related to the content, the questions and techniques must function as valid predictors of future performance. It is generally impos-sible to collect all relevant data, so the data that is collected must be representative, and must lead to a valid decision which reflects the decision that would be made if all the relevant data were present.

Test what is taught. Your program is designed to teach, simulate, or permit practice or decision making in a particular area, so collect data and make decisions based on that. If all your program does is teach someone how to identify and name the parts of a particular piece of machinery, don't design an assessment procedure on their ability to take the machinery apart and put it back together. On the other hand, don't just assess memorization.

Use equivalent items. Assessment items should be designed and written at the same level as the rest of the program. They should be equivalent, not identical to, example items presented by the program.

Test desired competency, not test taking ability. Competency based items should assess the ability of the learner to achieve the desired competency, not common sense, the ability to guess, or the ability to take tests.

Assess learning objectives, not teaching techniques. Design assessment items around your predetermined objectives, not based on the strategies you chose to present or achieve those objectives.

Make assessment techniques and questions fair. Avoid racial, sexual, cultural, handicapped, and other biases in the assessment process. Many times the way you write a question, or the context in which the assessment is conducted, will bias the results against a certain group of individuals. When testing your program, test it on audiences from a wide range of backgrounds, to assure that no bias exists in either the instructional or the assessment portion.

Don't make data collection more complex than the ability to prescribe solutions. It doesn't make any sense to collect information that will never be used. If the program, teacher, or learner can't or won't do anything with the assessment data, don't waste the learner's time or the computer's memory collecting it.

3.2 DIAGNOSIS AND PRESCRIPTION

Without a doubt, diagnosis and prescription are the two most difficult processes in designing an effective, individualized, computer based instruction program. There are few if any general rules on what a designer should do if a certain situation exists. Diagnosis and prescription must be based on a solid understanding of the anticipated audience, the learning process, instructional strategies, motivation techniques, and failure causes and—most

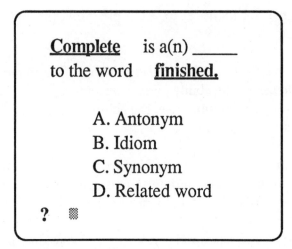

Figure 3.2   Diagnosing a problem based on response data

important—on a broad understanding of the subject matter covered by the program.

Diagnosis should not be a guessing game. It should be based on the decisions and data discussed in the previous section. Computer based diagnosis does not mean that the computer actually makes the diagnosis. Computers are not thinking, reasoning entities, they are machines that carry out instructions programmed into them by people. If diagnosis is going to occur in your programs, you have to establish the rules and instructions which the computer will carry out. To do this, you must first look at all of the information that the computer will be collecting; second, determine what that information might tell you about what is happening with the learner; and third, establish a set of rules that govern the computer's action under each of the anticipated conditions. Sounds like a lot of work, and it is, but it is the key to an effective individualized instructional program.

To illustrate how the process might work, let's look at a frame where a multiple-choice question was presented (see Figure 3.2). There are four possible answers, in this case "C" is the correct response and "A," "B," and "D" are distractors. Since our purpose is to make a diagnosis based on the available data, we first need to look at the possible responses the computer might receive in this instance. If the learner types in the letter "C" the diagnosis is simple. The learner knew the correct answer, so we diagnose that learning has occurred. We could of course group all the other responses as incorrect and diagnose that no learning occurred. But that would be too simplistic; instead, let's try to understand *why* the learner might have typed one of these other responses. One diagnosis might be that the learner had no idea what the correct response was and simply guessed incorrectly. On the other hand, the learner may have had some idea of the correct response. Each of the distractors has some relationship to the correct response. For example, antonym and synonym often get confused because they sound a lot the same and are often taught as opposites in the same lesson. A diagnosis for this response ought to be unique from the diagnosis used for either of the other two incorrect responses.

The four options provided are not the only data to consider. The learner may press the return/enter key; or type the word rather than the letter; or even choose to type a response other than the available options. These responses may indicate different types of problems that the learner is having with this question; and, as a program designer, you will have to decide whether to diagnose the problem and attempt to prescribe a solution or to ignore the problem and diagnose all incorrect responses the same.

With any luck, your failure analysis (i.e., analyzing a program to determine the most likely places where user failure may occur) and your subsequent program evaluation (i.e., evaluating the results gained through actual use of the program by the target audience) should indicate to you those places in your program where you should put your time and effort into improving specific diagnosis and prescription. As a designer, work closely with content experts, potential users, and others to establish a set of rules that anticipate as many response and decision patterns as possible.

Diagnosis is just half of the process. For each diagnosis you should try to come up with a prescription to correct the problem or to reward success. The purpose for a prescription is for you to accommodate the different needs of students by using the diagnostic data to match those needs to appropriate instructional solutions.

It should be pointed out that, in many cases, a computer based instructional solution may be neither reasonable nor possible. In these situations, the learner may be instructed by the computer to go to the teacher for additional help. Or the computer may provide a list of outside resources where the solution may be found. In the first instance, the program should provide the teacher with as much diagnostic data as possible to help them develop an appropriate prescription.

Prescriptions may be simple or complex. For some students, the solution may require the slowing down or speeding up of the presentation rate; for others, it may require a major remediation sequence to re-teach a concept, using different approaches with different examples. Experience, and your analysis of potential failure points, should suggest some solutions to most critical problems.

The important thing to remember when designing prescriptions is that you are attempting to get the right solution to the learner at the right time, and for the right reason. The right reason may be to improve the instructional process, to motivate an unmotivated learner, to improve the rate of progress, or to avoid unnecessary repetition. These and many other reasons will make the instructional process more efficient and effective.

To be effective, prescriptions must have a direct relationship to learning performance. They should inform learners what they need to learn and how to learn it. A learner may be told, for example, that the most recent response was incorrect and the learner should try it again to see if that solves the problem. In another circumstance, the learner may be informed that he or she passed the first two objectives of the unit; but that they need more practice on items covered by the third objective. Prescriptions don't and shouldn't always require special remedial program segments. If a simple prescription will do the job ("Take two aspirins and go to bed"), don't prescribe a major operation.

Prescriptions should recognize success as well as failure. If they only tell learners what hasn't been learned and what additional work they need to do, they may begin to believe that no progress is being made and perhaps they should give up. Learners need to know not only what they have learned but also what progress they are making.

Don't try to prescribe too much at once. Diagnosis and prescription should be an ongoing process. As soon as a problem or a need is diagnosed, it should be prescribed for them.

If the learner and the computer can eventually solve the instructional problem alone, don't involve the teacher. Learners are much more willing to work hard at solving problems when they know that only their ultimate success, not their failures along the way, will be reported to the teacher. Prescription is for the learner first, the teacher second.

The design of prescriptions should include some of the following factors:

Prescriptions should be understandable.   Don't make the cure worse than the problem. Prescriptions should be based on the learner's needs and what the learner can understand.

Prescriptions should be realistic.   Don't prescribe more than you are prepared to support. The complexity of the management component should be in direct relationship to the complexity of the instructional elements.

Prescriptions should be based on facts.   Don't anticipate a prescription before you have all the facts. Don't lock a learner into a prescription beyond the point at which the diagnosis was relevant. Because a learner has a problem with one section of a program should not lock the learner into the slow track on all segments of a program.

Prescriptions should be based on program objectives.   Learners may have a lot of instructional problems and needs that are going to affect their use of your program. You can't solve them all. Diagnosis and prescription should only be for those areas covered by your instructional objectives.

Involve the learner in the prescription process. Believe it or not, learners sometimes know what they need more than computers do. Providing a broad range of learner options, combined with carefully designed, specific feedback, may be the best prescription you can provide for many instructional problems.

3.3 RECORD KEEPING/REPORTING

If your program is going to be used in an institution that requires accountability, include some form of record keeping and reporting system.

Computers generally have two ways of recording and reporting information/data—in a section of its internal memory, sometimes called random access memory, and/or on an external storage device, usually a disk or tape system. Storage of data in the computer's internal memory is very temporary. When the computer system is turned off, or when another program is loaded into the computer, this memory is usually cleared and the information is lost.

Disk storage, on the other hand, is permanent. The information stays on the disk (until deleted according to special instructions). The only problem with storing data this way is that there must be room on the disk for all the data you want to store at any one time. If for example 30 students are going to be using your program, and you expect to store a lot of information on each learner; and you hope to store this information on the disk that already contains your program, there may not be enough room left to handle all the information. This is generally not a problem on larger mini and main frame computer systems. In fact, it is a real advantage in using these computers for computer based management delivery.

Deciding how to store the information you have collected

really depends on how you intend to use it and report it. If you use it strictly to control program flow while the program is being used, then all necessary information generally can be stored in the computer—to be erased when the program is over and the information is no longer needed. In some situations a single piece of information, e.g., the learner's current location in the program, may need to be stored externally so that the computer can refer to it when a learner returns to the program. As a general rule, when disk storage is used, save only the portion of the data that must be preserved for later use.

Sometimes teachers need information on scores, messages, and diagnostic data. If storage space exists on a disk, this information can be stored and accessed later. If permanent storage is not possible, the next best option is a printer attached to the computer which can print a copy of the information before the computer is turned off. The teacher could collect the printed sheets, or the learner could deliver the printed copy to the teacher's desk. A third option, although much less reliable, is to provide the learner with a worksheet which is used to hand copy the information from the computer screen. The obvious problem with this is that the student may not always copy the information correctly for one reason or another.

Because of limited storage and programming space, comprehensive management reports are not provided with most microcomputer based programs. When reporting procedures are included, they are generally limited to individual progress reports. Included in an individual progress report is information on:

- *Learner performance*—based on criterion assessment data, and relative/norm-referenced data, this provides the learner/ instructor with specific achievement scores.
- *Learning prescription*—descriptive information on lesson assignments, objectives, assigned skill level, and other prescription assignments which may have been made by either the computer or the teacher.
- *Current location and status*—describes what area of the program

the learner is currently working on, and lists the objectives where each criterion has and has not been achieved.

If this information is stored on disk, it is generally a good idea to limit access to the report generator in some way. The easiest way is by a special key, e.g., a "control" key, or key combination. Or a password may be established by the instructor, which can be changed from time to time. This would be the more secure way. When multiple learners are using the same disk where individual records are stored, it is sometimes a good idea to give, or let learners select and use a password each time they use the program. This will prevent learners from cheating, inadvertently destroying, or changing records stored for other learners.

Unless your program is specifically designed for personal home use, it is generally a good policy to include some form of record keeping and reporting function with each CBI program you develop. It will go a long way, both in helping instructors integrate your program into a total learning environment and in promoting the individualization of instruction.

3.4 SUMMARY

Managing the instructional process involves five major functions:

- *Assessment*—collecting individual and system performance information.
- *Diagnosis*—determining learner needs.
- *Prescription*—matching needs to instructional approach.
- *Record keeping*—maintaining performance records.
- *Reporting*—providing feedback of results.

Assessment systems focus on specific decisions which must be made in order to deliver the most efficient and effective amount of information and practice. Information can be collected in three categories: affective, cognitive, and psychomotor.

Designing an assessment system involves: determining the type of decisions and conclusions that are required, and the information that is relevant to making those decisions; selecting an instrument that will collect the relevant data; and establishing a set of rules for determining actions to be taken.

Management decisions relate to course management, learner performance, learning sequence, and selection of appropriate learning activities.

Data can be either normative or criterion based and may include: actual responses, competency standards, cumulative scores, time/rate data, prescription data, individualized assessment items, lesson labels, learner notes, and repetitive data.

Assessment should be as unobtrusive as possible. It can be accomplished either before or after instruction, or it can be embedded in the instructional system.

Diagnosis and prescription should be based on the data collected through the assessment process. The main purpose is to match the right instruction with the right person at the right time. There should be a direct relationship between learner performance and learning prescription.

Record keeping and reporting should benefit both the learner and the instructor. Typical reports will generally provide data on learner performance, learning prescription, and lesson status.

3.5 ISSUES AND ACTIVITIES

1. Ask a group of teachers what kinds of information they would like a computer based instructional lesson to provide. Ask a group of learners the same question. Design an assessment and report flowchart to show how the data could be collected and reported.
2. If you needed to know whether a learner was working at a color monitor or not, how would you have the computer ask the question? Does the question get the correct re-

sponse if the learner is working at a "green" or "orange" screen monitor?

3. Select a computer based instructional program that doesn't contain an obvious management component and design one for it.

4. Select an objective that can be tested using a multiple-choice question. Write two multiple-choice questions, each having four possible answers. Only one answer should be correct, but each of the other answers should help you identify a particular problem the learner may be having. Describe the diagnosis/prescription process you could use for each of the incorrect responses.

5. Show a group of students a computer based instructional program that doesn't contain a management component. Discuss with the students the type of information they wish the computer had collected and the form they would like the data reported back in.

3.6 REFERENCES

Burke, R. L. *CAI Sourcebook*. Englewood Cliffs, NJ: Prentice-Hall, 1982.

Dick, W., & Carey, L. *The Systematic Design of Instruction*. Glenview, IL: Scott, Foresman & Co., 1985.

Gagné R. M., and Briggs, L. J. *Principles of Instructional Design*. New York: Holt, Rinehart & Winston, 1979.

Hofmeister, A. *Microcomputer Applications in the Classroom*. New York: Holt, Rinehart & Winston, 1984.

Hopkins, C. D., & Antes, R. L. *Classroom Measurement and Evaluation*. Itasca, IL: F. E. Peacock, 1978.

Kibler, R. J., Cegala, D. J., et al. *Objectives for Instruction and Evaluation*. Boston: Allyn & Bacon, 1974.

Payne, D. A. *The Assessment of Learning: Cognitive and Affective*. Lexington, MA: D. C. Heath, 1974.

Snow, R. E. Individual differences and instructional design. *Journal of Instructional Development*,(1)(1977).

Taylor, R. P. (ed.). *The Computer in the School: Tutor, Tool, Tutee*. New York: Teachers College Press, 1980.

4

Individualizing and Humanizing Computer Based Instruction

The important image is not the one on the screen, but the one in the user's mind.

Paul Heckel

4.0 INTRODUCTION

Every program you design is going to be different from every other program that you or anyone else designs. Each will be aimed at meeting a unique instructional need, and each will have its own unique set of objectives and apply its own set of strategies to meet those objectives. As unique as each program is, they should all have some things in common. They should all reflect a concern for the individual user and for meeting the needs of that user. That's what this chapter is all about; finding ways to make the computer more responsive, more "friendly," to the needs of the individual.

Sometimes we think of the computer as a totally unique instructional tool with nothing whatsoever in common with any other tool used in the instructional process. This is definitely not the case. Computers as processors of information are not that different from books, tape recorders, typewriters, or even chalkboards. There is a truism which can be applied to almost all media, "GIGO"—garbage in garbage out. The most frightening thing about designing for computers is the realization that the computer will not improve on the quality of your design. In fact, the design will probably get worse by the time it's programmed. The computer, like most other tools used in the instructional process, is really just an extension of your ability as a communicator.

From the point of view of the learner, your role as a designer of computer based communication is the same role played by a foreign language translator or interpreter. You understand the information that needs to be communicated to the learner, and it is your job to interpret that information; first, into a form that the learner can understand; second, into a form that the computer can utilize; and third, into a form that is as friendly as possible.

Meeting the communication needs of learners and at the same time meeting the computer's needs equally well is no simple task. One thing that makes it so difficult is the lack of personal contact between you and the learner. You don't have to face the puzzled looks or hear the maddening cries when your program fails to communicate. Because of this, as designers we sometimes forget that there are going to be real live people on the other end of that computer screen and that our first responsibility is to them, to "human engineer" programs to meet their interests, abilities, and needs.

4.1 HUMAN INTERFACING

Dr. Frank Gilbreth, who developed many of the principles that are applied to time and motion studies, proposed that, "It is cheaper and more productive to design machines to fit men rather than to force men to fit machines." Friendly human interfacing does this. Unlike the questions posed in earlier chapters, human interfacing is not so much what is being presented as how. The current trend toward highly structured programming languages has caused us to look carefully at the interval flow of programs and to apply complex structures to programs so that they will be easier to read and modify. Human interfacing implies that a similar effort should be undertaken on the external structure of our programs. This effort is not designed to benefit the programmer, but to help the learner perform complex tasks in the simplest, most familiar, and most meaningful way possible. Simplicity on the outside usually does not translate into a simple internal program. Generally just the opposite is true. Good human engineering requires designers and programmers to come up with complex program routines in order to simplify external processes.

Before you can design a computer program to meet the needs of people, you must first know something about the people you are writing for and the environment they will be using the program in. Knowing the content needs of the target audience is not enough. You need to know some things about users: their background in using a computer, their ability to function as an independent thinker and operator, their interests and attitudes toward computer based instruction, and so forth. Don't assume an "idealistic" learner, and especially don't assume that the user thinks, acts, and has the knowledge base that you have. Try to determine what a realistic user knows and doesn't know and, most important, what a user wants to know. Why will users be working with your program? How do they think, and what motivates them? What are their expectations from life and, specifically, from your program? If you are going to apply human interface principles to a program, you must know more about your audience than their intended use of your program.

The human interfacing standards you apply are going to depend on the environment in which your program is going to be used. Is your audience to be learners in a formal classroom, or will your program be an enrichment experience for learners relaxing at home? Will a teacher or some other knowledgeable person be close by? Are there any time constraints into which the program must fit? The audience analysis discussed in Chapter 1 should provide you with a profile of the learner's content needs. Many of your programs will have more than one user type. You may also need to develop a separate profile for the teachers or parents who will control the use of your program. The audience analysis will provide you with the essential background information you need to make human interfacing decisions.

Human interfaces are not made, however; they evolve. Once you know everything you can reasonably expect to know about your target audience, you still need to try out your program on real people as early as possible. How do they feel about the interfacing quality of your program? How do they react to the methods you use to control the interaction between the computer and the user? Base your final program design on the learner's knowledge, not your own.

Collecting data to adjust a program's human interface requires careful observation of users. Sometimes the best indicator of human interfacing problems is the user's body language. A puzzled look, squinting eyes, an extra long pause, and an incorrectly formatted response are all indicators of human interfacing problems.

4.2   FRIENDLY COURSEWARE DESIGN

We often hear, in reference to computer programs, the terms "friendly" and "unfriendly." What do these words really mean? In most cases, they describe whether or not the computer program allows users to function in ways that seem natural and intuitive to them. What seems "natural and intutive" to one individual, however, may not seem so to another. Fortunately, there are some things CBI designers can do to make computer based courseware appear friendlier to *all* users.

Friendly communication

Friendly courseware begins with friendly communication. When you write a CBI program, keep foremost in your mind the fact that you are writing to communicate with another human being. Even though it is the computer that is doing the communicating, the user should feel that the message was prepared by a friend for a friend. To be sure this comes across, you should generally write in the active voice. Put statements in positive form, especially feedback, and use concise, specific, concrete language. Think of the images you are creating in the mind of your user. Good communicators think visually, even when they use words as their medium. William Blake, the 18th-century English artist and poet, expressed this when he wrote:

> To see a World in a Grain of Sand
> And a heaven in a Wild Flower,
> Hold Infinity in the palm of your hand
> And Eternity in an hour.

The secret in creating such images lies in the ability to use what the learner already knows and to provide a constant interface between what is known and what is being learned. This can be accomplished by establishing a common ground, a shared experience, often by using similes and metaphors. Later in this book you will see how these writing techniques can also be used in CBI design.

Appeal to the senses.   All of our experiences and perceptions come through our senses. We are motivated when something appeals to more than one sense. CBI designers need to learn to use words, sounds, and graphics that cause the user to experience the various sights, sounds, smells, tastes, and feelings (touch) that are appropriate to a total learning experience. Select words that not only paint images but stimulate the senses as well. Friendly CBI design requires both creative communication and creative thinking.

Computer jargon distracts users who do not understand it. It is better to use language that is familiar to them. Short, specific, common words and ideas allow users to focus on information, not structure or vocabulary. We speak differently to our friends than we do to people we have just met. Courseware dialogues should be modeled after the former, the friendlier of the two styles. Communication should suggest a common understanding, background, interest, vocabulary, and need for information. Different programs require different forms of communications; therefore structure communication to match needs, functions, and problems that specific programs are intended to serve.

Friendly organization

Friendly courseware design has a sense of consistency about it. Each word, graphic, frame, and procedure adds to the shape of what has come before and what will come after.

Each element should serve a specific function, meet a specific need. Computer programs are rarely used to gain a general overview. Users are almost always looking for something specific. Your responsibility is to organize the program to meet their specific expectations.

The basic unit of any CBI program is the frame; therefore friendly courseware design begins with friendly frames. Each frame should present one—and only one—thought, idea, or problem. We humans learn best if we can focus on just one thing at a time. Friendly software helps. So avoid enormous blocks of print, or packed frames of print and/or text. Don't make frames so short that context is lost, or so long that learners are overwhelmed. Design and write frames that sound natural. Don't permit content or design to mask the purpose of the frame.

The beginning of a new frame should signal a new step in the development of the subject. Transition from frame to frame is extremely important if the learner is not going to get lost or confused in the process. Frames should include information that aids the learner in this transition along with the other information that is eesential to the frame. Frames that have similar ideas should be designed the same way. Then the learner can see the similarity of content and purpose among them. Keep related frames together and related graphics together with explanations. There is nothing so frustrating as getting lost, whether in the middle of an unfriendly, unfamiliar city or an unfriendly, unorganized computer program. Learners must always be aware not only of where they are and where they've been in a program but also where they're going and how to get there. Have a vision of your program with all of its parts in place, then design it so that the user has the same vision.

Don't let users get lost in a sea of details. To clearly comprehend the operation of the program, they only need to see those parts of it that directly relate to their purpose for using it.

Be consistent! Once the user learns the routine for moving from frame to frame, don't change it just for the sake of change. Provide a simple user interaction technique to meet an intended function, then stick with it. Use a common-sense approach. If you need to assign a key to perform a specific function, e.g., erase or edit a response, don't select one that has nothing to do with the function, or one that is difficult to remember. Instead, use a key that has some relationship to the function, e.g., the "E" key for "edit."

User control

Users want to feel that they are in control at all times. Engage the user. Let users know the degree and nature of the control they have over the learning environment; for example, how to stop the program, how to repeat a frame or group of frames, how to get help if needed, even how to move on when they are ready. Don't waste a learner's time on unnecessary activities. Friendly courseware realistically assumes that users are not interested in the program, only in getting their work done. So every word, graphic, and procedure you include in your program should make it quicker and easier for users to do so. You may have seen a neat programming technique or instructional procedure. Don't include it in your program unless it serves a useful purpose for the user. Users need to focus on the instructional task, not the mechanism for accomplishing it.

Menus and other techniques described later in this book allow users to see what options are available and easy to make. Make it easy for learners to browse. Many of them need to have an overall image of what the whole program is going to provide them before they can settle down to one specific lesson. One reason most of us find books such a friendly medium is that we can move freely through its contents. Designers should provide only as much structure to a program as is absolutely necessary.

Friendly information input and output

The learner shouldn't have to guess what response the computer is waiting for, or what format the response is supposed to follow. The learner may not know the correct answer to a question, but should never have to wonder about what kind of response or interaction the computer is waiting for, how that response is to be entered into the computer, when the appropriate time is for making a response, or where the response will appear or be utilized. Except for things like passwords, always show on the screen what the user is typing, and let users know that the computer is responding to their input.

Most people are better at recognizing a correct response than they are at recalling one. Wherever appropriate, provide users with available choices, rather than asking them to generate one. "Which lesson?" is a question frustrated learners ask when they have no idea what the names of the lessons are. Not knowing that you are supposed to press the space bar to continue can cause a learner enough anxiety to quit the program altogether.

The computer provides information to learners, but learners need to know how to find it. Information should be delivered in a form and using language that users can understand and utilize. Communication between the users and the computer should be convenient for the user, not the computer.

Make it work

Learners should feel confident that the program will not stop operating just because they hit a wrong key or enter an incorrect response. CBI designers should assume that Murphy's law—what can go wrong, will—was written especially for them. Friendly courseware design anticipates problems. It doesn't leave it up to the user to solve them when they occur. If you're not sure a particular procedure or piece of instruction will work, then don't use it. Find a better way. Programs should be designed to work under the worst condition, not the best. It is said that Napoleon gave his battle orders to an idiot to read before he presented them to his generals. If the idiot could understand them, he felt fairly safe that his generals could. Before we release our programs, it would not be a bad idea to let our materials be reviewed by individuals with less than the anticipated background of our intended users. Many times, the only way you will ever know if a program really works is to test it out on those for whom it was intended. When you do, don't argue when they tell you they are having problems with it. Your job is to make the program work the way the user hopes it will, not make the user function the way you want.

Anticipate problems. Give learners time to catch their own errors before their input is accepted by the computer. Have the user press the enter key first. Then, after the input has been entered into the computer, have the computer check to see if the input is logically correct before processing it. In most instances, check for intent and ideas, not grammer and spelling (except of course where grammer and spelling are essential parts of the lesson). Where errors are found, provide friendly error messages which inform learners what changes to make. Never make learners feel that an error message is an evaluation or a personal attack on their ability or intelligence. Don't make them defensive. Anticipate why learners might give a particular incorrect response, and provide enough information to allow them to correct the problem. If the computer can correct the problem without additional input from the user, let it do so. For example, if learners forget to capitalize their name when they type it in, have the computer do it for them; don't play unnecessary games with the user.

When major branching decisions are being made, based on a user's input, reinforce and allow the user to undo that action before the action is executed. For example, say a user can cause the computer to print a display screen by pressing a particular function key. After the key is pressed, it is helpful for the user to see a confirming statement such as "Print the current screen (Y or N)?"

Be specific in your program instructions. Asking a learner to enter the "File name" is not nearly as useful as, "From the list of lessons shown above, type the name of the lesson you wish to start with and press the enter key." Your instructions should anticipate how a learner could get lost, lose interest, or misunderstand. As a rule, it is better to provide too many instructions than too few.

Anticipation is better than remediation. It is far more efficient and effective to anticipate and avoid problems than it is to have to figure out solutions later on. A large number of remediation routines is usually a sign that the planning and testing of the original program was inadequate. Friendly programs make it possible for users to do it right the first time, rather than correct mistakes later on.

Information/program match

Programs should do what they say they will do, no more, no less. Don't advertise more than you can deliver. The documentation that comes with your program should describe exactly what occurs in it. Don't leave in it any "undocumented features" that are going to surprise the learner when they are discovered, or that are going to cause the program to crash when they are not.

Let form follow function

There is a long-standing rule in CBI design that "form should follow function." Design forms should be appropriate, "obvious" to the message and material being communicated. Programs that require users to continually look back at the manual are not user friendly. When we read a book we don't need a second book to tell us how to move back a page or go to the index. A friendly computer program is just as easy to use. A well-written user manual is an appropriate part of any courseware package, but it should not be used to cover up an unfriendly software design. The strategy of the programs, and the format of each individual frame, should both be appropriate to the purpose and function of the design. Let your program's form follow its function. Strike a careful balance between its artistic qualities that excite and motivate (form) and its meaningful messages and specific objectives (function).

Simplicity and efficiency

No matter how sophisticated, everyone appreciates someone who gets the information across in the simplest way possible. If you can teach a learner how to do something with one or two frames, don't design an entire simulation for it. Watch for opportunities to save user time and effort. If a choice or response can be made with a single key stroke, don't force the learner to type out the whole word or sentence, e.g., "Y" instead of "yes," or "1" instead of "Lesson 1—Nouns." Make the program easy to learn and easy to operate. Don't make learners remember rarely used information. Provide quick reference/help frames that make looking up the rarely used information easier than remembering it.

Variety

People enjoy and need variety to stay alert and aware of what's going on around them. Be consistent in most user interaction requirements, but provide a variety of presentation and display techniques which are appropriate to the learner's abilities and interests.

Keep it moving

People hate to wait, especially if they don't know what they're waiting for. If something is going to take more than a couple of seconds for the computer to load or compute, then inform the user what's happening and approximately how long the wait will be. Use programming techniques that reduce the loading time for graphics and other files that must be loaded from an external storage system. Where possible, have the computer perform time-consuming processes while the user is involved with some other process, for example, reading the information on the screen, or determining the solution to a problem.

Additional techniques for friendly human interfacing will be covered below and in later chapters. Applying all of them, however, will still not guarantee the successful human interface of your program. Like the writer of a good novel, you must let your personality and your concern for the individual learner show through in the lesson material you prepare, in the question you write for the computer to ask, in the feedback you provide, and in every other aspect of the design and programming process. Before you do any CBI development, get to know your target audience as individuals with individual needs and interests.

4.3 INDIVIDUALIZED COMPUTER BASED INSTRUCTION

The term "individualized instruction" has come to mean many things to many people. For some, it means that every learner goes through the same materials, but each completes those materials at his or her own rate. To others, it means a particular medium, like a programmed text or computer; and to others it suggests a complex system of instruction which is personally designed and carried out according to each individual learner's needs, interests, and abilities. In this section we will examine some of the characteristics that typify individualized computer based instruction. You may not include all of them in your program, but you should consider all of them as possibilities.

Self-pacing

The rate of presentation of individual computer frames should be controlled by the learner. Individuals read at different rates, and they have other learning habits that affect how quickly they are ready to receive information. Frames should generally remain on the screen until the learner presses the space bar or some other control device to indicate they are finished and ready to move on.

The concept of self-pacing should be applied to larger portions of the program as well as to individual frames. Your program should require that learners be present for only the minimal amount of instruction necessary to master a given concept. Any instruction or practice that occurs beyond mastery should be optional.

Topic selection

Within some limits, learners should be allowed to select topics that they perceive as being most relevant or of immediate interest to them. Unless the learning map, discussed in chapter 2, indicates an absolute prerequisite relationship between sub-lessons, the learner should be allowed to select the topic and determine the preferred sequence of instruction. The content and presentation should be modified to fit the learner, not the learner modified to fit the content.

Learner initiated testing

Let learners determine when they are ready to take final criteria tests. The program should include options to repeat a lesson and/or gain additional practice, which can be accessed by the learner prior to the final criteria testing. The learner may fail to meet criteria on the first try. Provide a repeatable testing option with different but equal criteria test items.

Difficulty selection

If reasonable and appropriate, levels of difficulty should be selected by the learner. If not, they may be determined by a competency pre-test given on each required performance objective. In either case, the learner should not be locked into a particular learning level for an entire lesson but allowed to work at different difficulty levels depending on the the task or objective.

Individual performance testing

A learner's performance should be judged against a specific predetermined criterion. The standard may be one that has been established prior to a learner entering a program, or it may be one that is relative to that learner's previous performance on the program. In either case, judgement should be based on personal performance, not the performance of peers.

Remedial and enhanced instruction

Some individuals, for one reason or another, cannot master an objective after the initial presentation. Secondary instruction should be provided whenever possible. Don't repeat the previous instruction; approach the topic from a different angle, with a unique set of examples.

Learners who demonstrate a high proficiency for learning on a particular task could be provided with supplemental instruction which builds on normal required tasks. This saves them time waiting for slower learners to complete the regularly assigned instruction.

Instructional unit size

Instruction should consist of short activities which can be mastered within a 15- to 20-minute maximum time frame. This is realistic for a normal classroom and the attention span of most adult learners. Shorter lessons may be required for very young children.

Individualized delivery

One computer to one child is the preferred delivery system, except in situations where group dynamics may serve the instructional objective. When you design a program for use with small groups, you should allow for multiple responses to individual items. This encourages individual learners to respond and experience the learning task in their own unique way. Group competition should generally be discouraged, unless it encourages individuals to improve their own personal performance.

Meaningful interaction

All required responses and interaction with teachers should be meaningful to the learner, relate directly to the program's main objectives, and lead to increasingly higher and more difficult levels of achievement. Most learner/computer interaction should be for learner practice. Quality feedback from the computer should be part of each interaction. To make such feedback nonthreatening it should generally be provided only to the learner. Where possible, learners should be allowed to solve their own problems with the help of the computer. Only when necessary should they request help from a peer or the teacher. Generally, only the results of the final criterion test should be reported to the instructor.

4.4   STRUCTURING THE PROGRAM

This is not going to be a section on programming per se, but on some features to consider when programming, features that affect the human interface and "user friendly" quality of your program. The effort here is not to ascribe human qualities to the computer. A computer is a machine, and we should not kid ourselves or its users that it is anything but a machine. Some machines are easier to use than others. They seem to be able to respond to our needs. While other machines, it seems, are always trying to control us. In this section I will point out some things you can do in your program to teach computers to respond to people.

The first thing you need to remember, if you are going to have a user friendly program, is that users are not programmers. They don't understand, in many cases, how a computer works, and they definitely don't understand all the complexities involved in communicating with a computer in its language. A programmer may run your program with no problems whatsoever, but don't assume that the program is user friendly. It may present errors and problems to beginning users that are so minor that the average programmer wouldn't even give them a second thought. To the new user, however, it's a catastrophe.

Despite the fact that we humans are the most complex organism on earth, we like to do things in the simplest way possible. We become frustrated, and quite often we give up, when a task looks too difficult or too complex. One of the first things you can do to make your program more friendly is to make it look friendly.

- Provide straightforward information and ask straightforward questions.
- Don't create a maze out of the parts of your program; a way in, but no way out.
- Keep frame displays simple and use lots of empty space.
- Make frame displays aesthetically pleasing.
- Use the learner's name occasionally. People love to hear or read their own name. It makes the program seem more personalized to them.
- Keep the learner in control, but keep the program moving with the least amount of effort on the part of the learner.
- Don't make the user remember information that only relates to the program's operation.
- Don't force the learner to provide the computer with information that the computer is perfectly capable of figuring out for itself.

Programs should be designed so that they "feel" right. When you open a car door, or turn on the hot water for a bath, or even turn on a light switch, there seems to be a natural, familiar way of doing it. When someone reverses the door or switch, it takes extra effort and time to figure out the new system. Computer programs should make use of the natural, intuitive actions of people. Computer program designers have developed, over the years, unwritten standard procedures for inputting and outputting information, e.g., press the Return/Enter after typing in a response. Observe other CBI programs, and use the same standard procedures. If you're not sure where to place something on the screen, or what type of response to require from a user, ask a friend who knows nothing about the computer to tell you where they would expect to find the information, or how they would like to respond.

Anticipate user needs and problems. Any time the program receives input from the learner, ask yourself: "What can possibly go wrong at this point?" Keep the learner informed with useful information. "Syntax error" doesn't tell the learner anything about the problem. Messages provided to learners should be written in a language that learners understand and that help learners overcome the problem. Problems that might be encountered before the program begins should be anticipated in the documentation that accompanies the program.

The chapters on frame design and screen formatting will describe some specific actions you can take to make these elements of your program more friendly and effective. The following are some things you can do. Although they generally don't show up on the screen, they can have a real impact on the way the program runs.

4.5 CRASHPROOFING PROGRAMS

As long as learners always hit the right key, or type the right response, most computer programs seem to run just fine. It's when the computer receives a response that it doesn't expect that the real test of a program begins. The process of checking for, and handling, unanticipated actions is generally referred to as "crashproofing" a program. The following are some of the things that your program should be designed to watch out for, and to overcome when they occur.

Check response size

Most computers have a maximum size of response they can accept without the user pressing the Return/Enter key. Most responses also have a normal response length. For example, if you ask the learner's age, you can anticipate that the response will contain no less than one character and no more than three characters (0–999). There are ways to check the length of a response to see if it fits into the limits which the computer or a normal response would require. Using these techniques throughout your program will allow you to identify certain user problems before they go too far.

Checking for a lack of response

The lack of an input when one is requested, i.e., the learner simply pressing the Return/Enter key with no other response, may not cause an immediate problem. But one may occur later when the program tries to use the expected input and can't find it. Failure to respond should be identified immediately, so that the learner doesn't have to repeat major sections of the program to solve the problem.

Eliminate excess response data

It is a common practice in CBI and other programs to require the computer to determine if a user's response matches exactly a preprogrammed set of characters. Unfortunately, it is also common for learners to type extra spaces before and/or after the correct response. The extra spaces can cause the computer problems if they are not eliminated before the computer judges the response. Most programming languages provide ways to eliminate and shorten learner responses to just the required elements.

Check response types

Computers treat numbers that are to be used mathematically in a manner different from all other characters or inputs it can receive. Because of that, it must be told what type of input to watch for. If it receives a type of input that it is not expecting, the program can stop operating. It is possible to structure a program so that it edits or modifies inputs to meet the anticipated type. In situations where this is not possible, it is always possible to test inputs for their correct type and to notify learners of the specific problem, thereby preventing normal program failures.

Provide a way to exit

Most programs should provide an exit option. Since exiting a program in the middle may be detrimental to the program itself, you should plan for this to be more than a single step process. Before the program is actually terminated, the learner should be warned that they are about to exit the program, and they should be given the option to return to where they left off. It is also a good idea for them to type out a word like "quit" or "end," instead of just entering a single key stroke. Single keys are easy to hit by mistake, but letter-word combinations are rarely typed by mistake.

Permit learner initiated corrections

Most times, if allowed, learners will identify their own mistakes and correct them. If a learner has already pressed the Return/Edit key, or if the computer accepted a single letter response without waiting for the Return/Edit key, this may not be possible. It is recommended that, before the response is accepted by the computer, a final act—such as pressing the Return/Edit key—should be required. Even if the response is as simple as a "Y" for "yes" or an "N" for "no," the learner should have the opportunity to review and change the response before the computer locks it in.

Let the computer do as much of the work as possible

When corrections are required, the learner need only correct that portion which contains the change. Let the computer retype the rest, if necessary.

Check and handle unexpected errors

Many problems that cause the computer to fail cannot be specifically identified or handled. For these, you will need to build what is commonly called an "error trapping" or error handling routine into your program. Error handling routines should serve two major functions: they should allow the program to recover if some unexpected problem does cause the normal flow of the program to be terminated; and they should provide meaningful messages which help the learner identify the problem and correct it when given a second try. Merely descriptive messages like "BAD SUBSCRIPT" or "OUT OF DATA" or "FILE NOT FOUND" are worthless to the average user. Better to tell the learner, "The file you have requested is not available in either of the disk drives. Check to see if you have the correct disk in the drive, or type 'CATALOG' to see a listing of the available files." It means a bit more reading for the learner, but is far more informative. Error messages such as this should tell the learner as specifically as possible what caused the problem and should offer a possible solution. Provide both pieces of information in language the user will understand, not computer gibberish.

4.6   QUESTIONS AND FEEDBACK

A key element of human interfacing is the interaction that takes place between the user and the computer. Learner interaction can be broken down into three functions: questions, input, and feedback.

Questioning techniques

When we think of asking questions in an instructional environment we generally mean questions used in the testing process. Questions in a CBI program, however, serve many purposes. They are used to get a learner's name, to indicate a lesson choice from a list of options, and to set margins on a printer. The quality and accuracy of the information given in response to a question are directly related to the quality of the question itself.

Learners should never have to guess what the program wants them to do. Questions should be concise; but they should state exactly what kind of information the computer is seeking and what format to use in inputting the information.

Structure questions and required responses so that typing is kept to a minimum, unless the learning objective requires a more extended form of performance. Even then, the learner should type as little as possible.

Make sure the question fits the objective and the desired response. A question like "What is the force?" may get you a response that better fits into a course on the movies than a course in physics. The question should be in context with other events that have just transpired in the program. Avoid questions that are off the wall, as the saying goes.

When you ask a question, leave enough room for the answer, and let the learner see the answer as it is being typed. When nothing happens on a screen, learners assume that the computer is broken and that their response is not being accepted.

The question and the response should be together. Don't type the question at the top of the screen and then have the learner's response recorded at the very bottom of the screen. The learner's response should appear immediately following the question, on the same line if possible.

When the question requires more than a simple response, provide a sample. Don't permit the response to get too complex.

If you think the learner will get confused while formatting a multiple part question, then divide the question into shorter, single-answer questions.

Ask questions that require thought, not just copying or repeating back what has just been said. A question like, "What color is a blue sky?" may seem ridiculous, but many such questions asked by CBI programs are not much better.

The difficulty level of questions should be appropriate to the learning capacity of the user. If the learner can't read, it's ridiculous to say, "Type in your first name and press the RETURN key." The single-word question "NAME?," while abrupt, may get the desired response where the complete sentence would not.

Ask questions that will result in predictable responses. A question like, "How does the philosophy of capitalism compare with that of communism?" leads to a response that is difficult for a computer to handle. Save this type of question for a classroom discussion. Better to ask the learner, "Place a '1' next to each of the following words that describes a capitalistic society, and a '2' next to those that describe a communistic society, and a '3' next to those that describe both." This permits the computer to assess whether or not the learner can make the anticipated comparison. Computers can't get at every type of question that needs to be asked. Ask only those that will elicit a response that results in meaningful feedback from the computer.

Response and input handling

Asking the right question should result in the computer getting the "right" answer. Determining what the right answer is is not as easy as it sounds when a computer is involved. In an earlier section it was pointed out that even the presence of a few extra blank spaces can cause the computer no end of problems in determining if a response is a preprogrammed item. At the same time you are designing the questions you will need to give some thought to the types of answers you are going to allow the computer to accept as correct, partially correct, or incorrect.

With specially designed peripheral devices and interface units, computers can receive and analyze numerous forms of input. Voice, music, touch, and input from light-sensitive pens are just some of the newer forms of input currently being perfected which will have great impact on future CBI programs.

Standard input types can be classified five ways:

- *Single key*—including the Space Bar and Return keys as well as individual symbol keys.
- *Multiple choice*—input selection based on a list of options or question choices.
- *Free-word entry*—input of one or two words which the learner must generate with limited prompting by the computer.
- *Constructed text*—variable-length responses which are generated by the learner. May be as long as several pages in length.
- *Coordinate responses*—generally inputted through devices such as "game" paddles, graphic tablets, a "mouse," touch-sensitive screen, etc. The input is considered by the computer as a series of numeric coordinates which can be used to identify specific x and y screen or tablet locations. These same coordinates can then be associated with visual images—including words—which are located at that relative position on the screen or tablet for identification, selection, or processing.

Response judging

One of the easiest ways to solve many of the problems we have with learner responses is to limit the amount of information the learner is required to provide. In a multiple-choice question, for example, if the learner is only required to type in the letter, rather than a five- or six-word answer, the chances of typing and spelling errors being included in the response are greatly reduced. Single-letter/number or single-word responses are by far the easiest forms of responses for the computer to handle.

In instructional programs, spelling causes the greatest difficulty in learner interaction. When spelling is an important aspect of the instructional objective it should be checked and considered as part of the response. Where spelling is not a critical element, a great deal of damage can be done to the learning process if the computer tells the learner that the response was incorrect if the only thing incorrect was the spelling of the word. Once a correct concept or principle is unlearned because of incorrect feedback, it is much more difficult to re-teach the concept and have it stick with any level of confidence.

Two solutions successfully used to solve this dilemma are: to structure the program so as to judge the response correct but show the learner the correct spelling; or to provide a list of misspelled words at the end of the program. These options require advanced planning on the part of the CBI designer.

Questions that require a multiple-input response can sometimes cause problems for the computer and the CBI designer. As suggested earlier, these should generally be divided into a series of shorter questions, each requiring a single short input. If you choose to take this approach, it is sometimes a good idea to present all of the separate questions on the screen at one time and then move the input point (cursor) down the screen as each succeeding question is responded to. This technique helps to prevent learners from typing in related responses that they are afraid they won't have the opportunity to give. Suppose for example, you want a learner to input date of birth and you ask first for the "Day of birth?" The computer will probably be given the full date. But if you ask for:

Date of birth:
   Day:
   Month:
   Year:

it is much more likely that you will get the information in the form you want.

When single-key input is provided, you can expect learners to match exactly the response anticipated by the program. Never assume that just because the learner didn't type "Y" or "yes" that they must have typed "no." If you are going to require the learner to interact with the computer, then you should plan to handle each response as carefully as you would if you were sitting there listening to the response yourself.

When free-word entry responses are asked for, you must provide the computer information on how to handle synonyms, related words, abbreviations, misspellings, and homophones (words that sound alike). As a general rule, attempt the response yourself, and allow the same degree of variance in response that a live teacher would allow.

Most computers treat upper and lower case letters differently. If the computer is looking for a perfect match, and the learner has responded with a different upper/lower case combination than that which was preprogrammed in, the computer generally will determine that no match exists. It is possible to tell the computer to convert all the letters of a learner's response to either upper or lower case before any comparisons are made. The programmer then only has to provide a matched response in the converted case. This is an easy solution to the problem, but, like so many easy solutions, it doesn't happen unless the CBI designer and programmer make it happen.

One way that has been used effectively to solve some of the problems discussed above is to have the computer check a portion of the learner's response. Does the learner's response begin, or begin and end, with the correct letters? Another general indicator is the length of the response. The computer can determine the number of characters in a word and/or the number of words in a response. By having the computer look at both length and critical portions of the response it is often possible to handle misspellings, abbreviations, and homophones with a fairly high degree of accuracy.

Responses requiring more than a couple of words are by far the most difficult input for most computer systems to handle. Learners should not be expected to second guess the way a particular CBI designer would phrase an answer. Unless the required input is supposed to be a direct quote, it is difficult to anticipate all possible correct word arrangements in a long phrase input.

One possible solution is to have the computer scan long

phrases for key words. Most computer languages provide such an option, but they generally require that, if multiple keywords are evaluated, a definite order be applied to the search; that is, the words in the learner's response must appear in the same order as those that have been set up in the computer match instruction. Even though other words may appear between the match words, this limitation still prevents the computer from checking randomly ordered multiple responses.

When the computer is unable to judge the accuracy of a learner's response, it is often possible with older learners to have them judge their own response. In this situation, the computer, after receiving a response, would provide the learner with an approximate version of the correct response. Learners could then indicate to the computer whether they felt their response included the same general idea. The computer could then branch according to the judgment indicated by the learner.

Where younger children are involved, it may be necessary to store constructed responses on a disk so that the instructor can judge these responses at a more convenient time. The teacher would then have to inform the learner directly or through an "electronic mail" system about the result of his/her evaluation.

Response judging by a computer may be one of the most important and difficult parts of designing a CBI program. Unlike the human teacher, computers have a great deal of trouble handling even the most minor exceptions to the rule, unless they are preprogrammed to handle them. Your job as a CBI designer will be to anticipate every *reasonable* response and to decide how the computer is to handle each unique situation.

Feedback

Teaching the computer to analyze and judge a learner's response is only half the process. The computer must also be told what to do and what to feed back to the learner once the accuracy of the response has been determined.

The feedback provided a learner should always enhance or reinforce the learner's prior knowledge. If the learner's response is correct, the feedback should lead the learner to additional instructional experiences. If the learner's response is incorrect, the feedback should lead to discovering why it was incorrect, and what the learner needs to do to make it correct on the next attempt. Feedback should never put down learners, or make them feel that it is worthless to continue with the instructional experience.

Whenever possible, feedback should be specific and directly related to the response provided by the learner. Where possible, your CBI design should try to determine what kind of misunderstanding is causing the learner to make the incorrect response, and then provide a unique remedial sequence for each type of wrong answer.

Feedback should provide information on the form of the input as well as the accuracy of the response, i.e., misspelled words, commas required between responses, extra spaces, and so on.

Even when an unanticipated response is received, the computer should be programmed to provide feedback that fits the circumstance. A response like "That's not one of the answers I have on my list. Why don't you try again?" can fit a number of situations and still inform the learner as to the problem the computer is having judging the learner's input.

One of the most common forms of handling incorrect responses is to simply recycle the learner through the same question. This is effective in some cases but should never be done without first informing the learner that the first response was incorrect. If the item is a practice item, it is also a good idea to provide the learner with an additional "hint" before allowing a second try.

One slight variation on the above approach is to restate or reformat the question in a modified way for the second try. Sometimes it is the way the question is worded that is causing the problem and not the ability of the learner to respond to the question once it is understood.

It is generally a good idea when repeating a question to leave the learner's original response on the screen. Responses should be left on the screen while the feedback to that response is being provided. This helps establish a relationship between the two elements and allows the learner to analyze their response to see if, in fact, the computer did judge it correctly.

Never allow a learner to become trapped into an endless loop of wrong answers with no way of escape. Generally, learners who can't get the correct response within the first couple of tries are guessing. They should be sent to some type of remedial sequence where the misunderstanding can be resolved.

Feedback should be informative and motivating but not overly time consuming. Feedback that includes "flashing lights and whistling bells" are all right once in a while, but they generally waste a lot of time and slow the pace of the program for fast learners. They also lose their effectiveness if they are used too often.

While we're on the subject of flashing lights, etc., don't make the feedback that is provided for an incorrect response more exciting than that provided for a correct response. A frowning clown face can sometimes be more fun than a smiling clown face. You don't want your learner to give incorrect answers just to see the feedback.

The elements that make up learner interaction, i.e., questioning, input, and feedback, are some of the most important parts of any CBI program. It takes time to figure out a better response than just "Correct" or "Incorrect," but it will add to the overall instructional value of your program for learners.

4.7 SUMMARY

Designing computer programs that meet the needs of individual learners should be the goal of all CBI programs. Programs should provide for learner control over the computer system and the learning environment. Programs should be individualized by providing for:

- Self-pacing
- Individualized topic selection

* Learner-initiated testing
* Variable entry and difficulty levels
* Remedial and enhanced instruction
* Individualized delivery systems
* Meaningful interaction

Programs should be structured around the way people operate, and they should require the computer to assume most of the responsibility for interfacing with people. Programs should be made to look and act "friendly." Programming techniques should be used to prevent programs from stopping because of inadvertent actions or misunderstandings on the part of the learner. This can be done by:

* Checking a learner's response for length and content
* Preventing incorrect keys from being pressed or affecting the program's performance
* Providing learner-initiated correction procedures
* Providing meaningful error handling and message routines

One of the key elements of any CBI program is the interaction between user and computer. Three important parts of that interaction are questions, response judging, and feedback provided by the computer.

Questions should be clear and concise and should require a minimal amount of typing. Questions should be formatted on the screen so that the question, response, and feedback can all be associated together in a proper relationship. Complex questions should be broken down into individual parts for ease and accuracy of response.

Responses to computer questions, or requests for input, can be classified in one of five categories: single key, multiple choice, free-word entry, constructed text, and coordinate response.

Asking the right question should result in the computer providing the right feedback. Response judging by the computer can be made more accurate if:

- Questions are specific, allowing for a limited range of correct responses.
- Questions requiring multiple answers are broken into parts, each part receiving only one portion of the answer.
- Spelling and other format issues are considered separately from the accuracy of the response itself.

Feedback by the computer should always be used to enhance or reinforce the learner's knowledge. It should be specific and directly related to the learner's response. Feedback for correct responses should be more interesting than feedback for incorrect responses.

4.8   ISSUES AND ACTIVITIES

1. Evaluate a few programs and list what you like and dislike about the way they treat you as a human being.
2. Observe a learner as he/she goes through a typical CBI program. Watch their "body language." See if you can identify points where they are having problems with the program just from the body actions you observe. Take notes and, when the learner is finished, verify your observations.
3. Make a list of what you feel represents the ideal relationship that should exist between a teacher and a learner. Translate that list into things the computer can do to emulate that condition.
4. Discuss with a computer programmer some of the concerns and issues raised by this chapter and see if together you can come up with programming techniques to solve the human interface problem.
5. Think about the role the teacher and/or parent will play in making a CBI experience more humanistic and individualized, and prepare a set of guidelines which could be provided with your courseware to these individuals.

6. Write 5 to 10 questions that require different types of response patterns. Write a set of rules for judging the accuracy of each response. Have a friend or colleague answer the questions in ways that make sense but that are not always correct. Evaluate how well your rules would help you (or a computer) judge and provide accurate feedback for each response.

4.9 REFERENCES

Arnheim, R. *Visual Thinking*. Berkeley, CA: University of California Press, 1969.

Arnheim, R. *Art and Visual Perception*. Berkeley, CA: University of California Press, 1974.

Badre, A. N., & Shneiderman B. (eds.). *Directions in human/computer interaction*. Norwood, N.J.: Ablex, 1982.

Baecker, R. Human-computer interactive systems: A state of the art review. In P.A. Kolers, M.E. Wrolstad, & H. Bouma (eds.), *Processing of visible language 2*. New York: Plenum, 1980: 423–443.

Bailey, R. W. *Human Performance Engineering: A Guide for System Designers*. Englewood Cliffs, NJ: Prentice-Hall, 1982.

Boies, S. J., & Gould, J. D. User performance in an interactive computer system. Proceedings of the Fifth Annual Conference on Information Sciences and Systems, 1971: 122.

Boies, S. J. User behavior on an interactive computer system. *IBM Systems Journal*, 1974: 2–18.

Bolt, R. A. *The human interface: Where people and computers meet*. London: Lifetime Learning, 1984.

Burke, R. L. *CAI Sourcebook*. Englewood Cliffs, NJ: Prentice-Hall, 1982.

Card, S. K., Moran, T.P. and Newell, A. *Tye psychology of human-computer interaction*. Hillsdale, N.J.: Lawrence Erlbaum, 1983.

Cuff, Rodney N. On Casual Users. *International Journal Man-machine Studies. 12*, 1980:163–187.

Davis, R.M. Man-machine communication. In C.A. Cuadra, Ed., *Annual Review of Interscience and Technology*, Vol. 1. New York: Interscience Publishers, 1966: 221–254.

Dreyfuss, H. *Designing for People*. New York: Viking Press, 1955.

Engel, S. E., & Granda, R. G. *Guidelines for Man/Display Interfaces.* IBM Technical Report TR 00.27200, Poughkeepsie, New York: IBM, 1975.

Edwards, B. *Drawing on the Right Side of the Brain.* Los Angeles, CA.: J. P. Tharcher, 1979.

Foley, J. D., & Wallace, V. L. The art of natural graphic man-machine conversation. *Proceedings of the IEEE, 62* (4), 462–471.

Foley, J. D., Wallace, V. L., & Chan, P. The human factors of computer graphics interaction techniques. *IEEE Computer Graphics and Applications,* No. 1984: 13–48.

Gilb, T., & Weinberg, G. M. *Humanized Input: Techniques for Reliable Keyed Input.* Cambridge, MA: Winthrop Publishers, 1977.

Gilbreth, F. B., & Gilbreth, L. M. *Applied Motion Study.* New York: The Macmillian Company, 1917.

Grignetti, M. C. and Miller, D. Modifying computer response characteristics to influence command choice. *Proceedings of IEEE Conference on Man-Computer Interaction.* London, September 1970: 201–205.

Hanks, K., & Belliston, L. *Design Yourself.* Los Angeles, CA: William Kaufmann, 1977.

Heckel, P. *The Elements of Friendly Software Design.* New York: Warner Books, 1982.

Jones, P. F. Four principles of man-computer dialogue. *Computer Aided Design, 10,* 1978: 197–202.

Kamins, S., & Waite, M. *Apple Backpack: Humanised Programming in BASIC.* Peterborough, NH: BYTE/McGraw-Hill, 1982.

Lakoff, G., & Johnson, M. *Metaphors We Live By.* Chicago, IL: University of Chicago Press, 1981.

Martin, J. *Design of Man-Computer Dialogues.* Englewood Cliffs, NJ: Prentice-Hall, 1973.

McKim, R. H. *Experiences in Visual Thinking.* Monterey, CA: Brooks/Cole, 1980.

Meyers, J., & Tognazzini, B. *Design Guidelines.* Cupertino, CA: Apple Computer, 1982.

Minnesota Educational Computing Consortium. *Designing Instructional Computing Materials.* St. Paul, MN: Author, 1982.

Olson, S., & Wilson, D. Designing computer screen displays. *Performance and Instruction Journal,* Feb. 1985.

Price, J. *How to Write a Computer Manual: A Handbook of Software Documentation.* Menlo Park, CA: The Benjamin Cummings, 1984.

Rubinstein, R., & Hersh, H. *The Human Factor: Designing computer systems for people.* Digital Press, 1984.

Shackel, B. (ed.). *Man/Computer Communication.* Volume 1, Maidenhead Berkshire, England: Infotech International Limited, 1979.

Shneiderman, B. *Software Psychology*. Cambridge MA: Winthrop Publishers, 1980.

Smith, D. C. Irby, Kimball, & Verplank. Designing the Star User Interface. *Byte, 7* (4) 1982: 242–282.

Smith, H. T., & Green T. R. G. (eds.). *Human interaction with computers*. London: Academic, 1980.

Smith, S. L., & Mosier, J. N. *Design Guidelines for User-system Interface Software*. Massachusetts: The Mitre Corporation (Prepared for Deputy for Acquisition Logistics and Technical Operations Electronic Systems Division, Air Force Systems Command, USAF, Hanscom Air Force Base, Massachusetts) 1984.

Snow, R. E. Individual Differences and Instructional Design. *Journal of Instructional Development*, (1) 1977: 23–26.

Strunk, W., & White, E. B. *The Elements of Style* (3rd ed.). New York: Macmillan Pub. Co., 1979.

Tesler, L. The Smalltalk Environment, *BYTE, 6* (8), 1981: 90–147.

Thomas, J. C., & Carroll, J. M. Human Factors in Communication. *IBM System Journal, 20* (2), 1981: 237–263.

5
Designing Management Frames

5.0 INTRODUCTION

Frame design is the process of organizing content and interactive materials into small presentation segments, which can be displayed on a single display screen.

Designing CBI frames involves more than just cutting and pasting content to make it fit on a screen. It involves the synthesis of all your previous decision and information gathering efforts into a final presentation format.

Frame design, like much of CBI design, had its beginnings with the early proponents of automated instruction via programmed textbooks. Many of the methods we still apply are based on the research findings of those early efforts, and for this we should not be apologetic. But we should recognize that the modern computer has provided us with capabilities not available to those early designers, and we should make use of these new capabilities in designing modern CBI frames.

Frames designed for traditional programmed texts were primarily static. Once written and printed, there was little that the designer could do to change each frame to meet individual needs short of using complex and time-consuming branching techniques. In contrast, the CBI designer is working with a highly dynamic medium where the computer can, if necessary, redesign each frame, taking into account learner responses and information needs. Each learner can be provided with a personal prescription for learning by receiving different frame content, and can interact with that content in ways not available to early program text designers.

The fact that the modern computer offers the CBI designer many new and powerful capabilities does not mean that they are easier to design for and utilize. Breaking away from the traditions of the past does not come easy. If we are ever to see the computer provide a unique contribution to education, we must begin to combine the traditions of the past with the capabilities of current and future technology. A new tradition of frame design should be based on a recognition of individual learner differences and the ability of the technology to respond to those differences. Frames designed for the computer should meet the needs of learners, not force learners to meet the needs of the computer or frame designer. It is hoped that the content of the next few chapters will stimulate CBI designers in this direction.

5.1 THE PEDAGOGY OF FRAME DESIGN

The dictionary defines pedagogy as the "science or art of teaching." The process of frame design is both a science and an art. The principles and methods used in frame design must be derived from a solid research background in proven teaching/learning practices and from a sense of intuition and anticipation into what will work best in a given situation.

One fundamental difference between CBI design and design for a normal teaching situation is generally the absence of the teacher when the lesson is being presented. This difference must be taken into consideration in every frame you design. Frames must contain all of the information a learner will require in order to successfully complete that frame, or provide directions on what the learner is to do if the frame cannot be successfully mastered.

Frames, in addition to other functions, should lead to learner interaction. This does not mean that every frame must elicit an overt response from the learner, but each frame should cause the learner to at least covertly process the information and associate the new information with previously learned information. Even though such covert processing may be taking place, it is recommended that no more than three frames be allowed to pass without some form of active, overt response. Pressing the space bar to continue is not considered an active, overt response in most situations.

"Electronic page turning" is not considered an appropriate application of computers. When designing CBI frames, you should provide only sufficient text material to bring about the desired interaction and competency. Frames should rarely exceed 100 words if being presented on a 40-column display screen, or 150 words on a 65-column or larger display screen. If large amounts of background text material are required prior to learner interaction taking place, it is strongly recommended that a supplemental printed text be provided. CBI frames should be limited to the highly interactive portion of the content.

Frames should be kept as simple as possible. The next chapter will discuss some of the limitations computer-generated video displays have in showing complex materials. A more important reason for keeping frames simple is that learners learn and remember more from simple frames. To illustrate this point, consider the poem "Mary Had a Little Lamb," which most young children can remember and recite. How popular would it be, or how many children would have learned this simple poem, if it had been written in the following form?

Mary was the legal owner of a diminutive potential sheep, whose haliberments were as innocent of coloring as congealed atmospheric vapor. And no matter where the ultimate destination of Mary's peregrinations, after infantile southward was positively certain to caper.

It shadowed little Mary to the local dispensary of knowledge on diurnal division ofttime, which was contrary to all written and unwritten precedents. At the sight of the miniature mutton gamboling gaily at the front of learning, there was a considerable mirth and disport in the ranks of the seminary attendants.

-Author unknown-

Simplicity also makes good economic sense for you as a CBI designer. It is suggested that CBI designers apply a "PAIN-TO-GAIN" ratio to frame design. This means that the work that a programmer or learner will have to put into a frame must be worth the gain that will be realized from that frame. A single frame which utilizes complex drawing and display arrangements can take as much as an hour to design and program. If the information is essential, then the time spent is worth it, but if it is not, then the frame designer should seek a simpler way of presenting the essential information. Each frame should be weighed to determine if the pain-to-gain ratio is positive, and if it is not it should be redesigned until it is.

Simple frame design does not mean that everything should be written or illustrated at an elementary level. Frame design should be appropriate to the anticipated learner's level of understanding. Reading level and illustrative style should be carefully analyzed ahead of time to determine if the frame can be understood and will motivate the learners for whom it is being designed. Dialogues should resemble personal conversations. The computer does not need to be provided with a name and human emotions. But it doesn't have to appear cold and unfeeling either. When we read a good novel we often become emotionally involved with the characters, because we realize that there is a warm, human, feeling author behind printer's ink and paper. The human quality of a CBI program should come from the human quality of its designer, and we should not try to hide our human side.

The type of interaction required of the learner should be carefully planned and tested to determine if it is appropriate to both the learner and the desired learning outcome. Interaction just for interaction's sake is not encouraged. A wide variety of frame interaction techniques should be identified and utilized by CBI designers. Multiple-choice questions are fine if the purpose of the interaction is to determine if certain facts can be recognized; but they are useless if you want to know whether a learner can manage a small business profitably, for example. Abusive language, language that questions the learner's intelligence, or patronizing language and approach should be avoided at all costs. Interaction and the feedback that results should encourage and motivate the learner, even if an incorrect response is encountered.

For many teachers who have become CBI designers, the computer is a relatively new and fascinating piece of technology. There is a real danger in letting our fascination with the technology get in the way of good, sound instructional practices. The decisions on frame design should be based on learning needs, not in response to the computer and its abilities or limitations (more often, our understanding of those limitations).

This author has found that, if you define carefully enough what you want the frame to present, and if you select the right programming language and push the programming process hard enough, there are very few things that the computer cannot be made to do. In those situations where the computer cannot present the frame as you designed it, there is almost always some other device or teaching technique which can be interfaced with the computer to make the desired outcome possible. The important point to be learned is, don't let the computer control design. Let learning control all aspects of CBI design including the design of individual CBI frames.

Each frame that is included in a CBI lesson should serve a particular function in helping the lesson meet its overall objective. The form that a frame takes should follow the function which that frame is to serve. The frame functions, and the appropriate formats to use to achieve those functions, are the major topics that follow in this chapter. Keep in mind, while reading these sections, that individual frames do not generally exist in a vacuum. CBI designers must continually ask themselves not only "Does this frame work the way I want it to?" but "Is it functional within the context of other related frames, lessons, and the instructional environment as a whole?"

5.2 ORIENTATION FRAMES

Almost every program you design will begin with a frame or series of frames which we'll refer to as "orientation" frames. The main function of this type of frame is to tell the learner where he or she is in the program and to provide background information and help on the program's operation. The initial orientation frame is generally a title frame.

Title frames

A title frame, as the name implies, informs users of the title of the lesson they are about to begin. Title frames should be used at the beginning of individual lesson modules as well as at the beginning of the major lesson. The title should be descriptive of the lesson content. If the current lesson is broken into subunits, then the title should include both the main title and the subunit title for the current module and/or disk.

The appearance of the frame should be attractive and motivational, but designers should not attempt to get so clever with the title that they lose their ability to communicate the nature of program. Figure 5.1 shows an example of a main title frame.

In addition to the lesson title, the main title frame should also include a copyright notice. Under current copyright laws, it is not necessary to file for copyright to establish an author's exclusive rights to control how the work is used. Copyright protection exists from the moment a work is created in fixed form. However, to legally establish copyright, an appropriate copyright notice must be placed on the title frame of the computer program, the diskette label, and the first page of any accompanying printed documentation. This will establish the copyright holder's right to protection

Figure 5.1   Main title frame

for up to five years. For longer copyright protection, appropriate forms must be filed with the Copyright Office in Washington, D.C. Figure 5.1 includes the necessary copyright information in the bottom center of the frame. The information required for this purpose includes the words "Copyright" or the copyright symbol (©), i.e., the letter "C" with a circle or box around it, the date when the material was first copyrighted (this may include just the year or the month and year), and the name of the copyright holder. "All rights reserved" or "May be licensed for copying" or some other appropriate remark describing the conditions of copyright are generally included with the copyright information. While copyright protection is granted under the procedures described above, it may not be enforceable for damages unless a copyright notice is registered. For additional information on how to do this, write the Copyright Office, Library of Congress, Washington, D.C. 20559.

Don't include information on the title page which may change from time to time. If you are not planning on publishing your programs through a well-established company, don't include an

Figure 5.2   Title frame with multiple credits

address or phone number that may be changed during the usable life of the program.

If credits are required for some of the materials used in writing the program, or for the use of registered trademarks, this information should be included on the main title frame or a secondary title frame immediately following the main title frame. Figure 5.2 illustrates a slightly more complex title frame containing secondary copyright credits.

Many CBI authors are unaware that most programming languages require licensing before programs published in these languages can be sold. Most languages and program development utilities, i.e., graphic/illustration programs, require a credit line stating who the copyright holder is for that language or program. CBI designers should acquaint themselves with the current status and requirements associated with a programming language or programmer's utility before designing the title frames.

CBI designers should also be aware that many companies have obtained certain legal rights to the use of their name and logo or other major symbols. If the name or a registered symbol is used any place on a frame or diskette label, advance permission should be obtained for its use and a notice of the registered status included on a title or credit frame.

When permission is granted, a (®) superscript should be placed immediately after the first use in any program, advertisement, or label of the registered trademark. A credit line such as "Apple is a registered trademark of Apple Computer, Inc.", as illustrated in Figure 5.2, may also be required by the trademark holder.

The best rule is to ask permission and understand your rights and responsibilities before you include or use materials that may be covered by copyright or trademark laws. Companies are very sensitive about the misuse of their name, logo, and other materials. They will bring a lawsuit against individuals and companies that infringe on their rights, so protect yourself from the beginning.

Acknowledgments and other nonessential credits should be placed on an optional secondary frame. Learners should not be forced to spend large amounts of time looking at materials that are not required or directly relevant to the main functions of the lesson. It is recommended that the main title page not remain on the screen longer than 10 seconds and, correspondingly, that it should not include more material than can be read within that time frame.

Goal and objective frames

The major purpose of a CBI lesson is to assist learners to learn. Experience has shown that one of the most effective ways of helping learners to learn is to tell the learner what he or she is supposed to be learning. In most CBI programs, objective frames should be available at the beginning of each new lesson, lesson unit, or lesson module to tell the learner what he/she is supposed to learn from the lesson, drill-and-practice, or simulation that follows. If a number of goal and objective displays are utilized at a single point in the lesson, it is advisable to make the viewing of these frames optional.

Many CBI programs will be used over and over by a single

```
 _____
|   _____   |
|  | English  Grammer:  Parts  of  Speech | |
|  |_____| |
|     At the completion of this unit you    |
|     should be able to:                    |
|  *  Define noun, pronoun, adjective, verb,|
|       adverb, preposition, conjunction,   |
|       interjection.                       |
|  *  Give three or more examples of each   |
|       part of speech.                     |
|  *  Identify each part of speech in a     |
|       sentence context.                   |
|                                           |
|   This unit should take you approximately |
|   15 minutes to complete.                 |
|      Press the SPACE BAR to begin...       |
|_____/
```

Figure 5.3 Goal/objective frame

learner. Once the learner has identified the objectives of the program, they should not have to sit through those frames again. On the other hand, the current objective frames should be available to the learner from within a lesson. As a lesson progresses, many learners like to look back at lesson objectives to orient themselves as to why the lesson is developing the way it is. This may be accomplished by assigning a function or help key as an access key to the currently active objective frame(s).

The lesson objective(s) should be stated in such a way that the learner will know, when they finish the lesson segment, whether they can meet the stated objectives. Every frame that follows the goal and objective frame(s), and all required learner interaction, should be used to make the achievement of the objective(s) possible.

Figure 5.3 shows an example of an objective frame. In addition to the statement(s) indicating the current CBI objectives, the frame may and generally should contain some indication of the approximate amount of time it will take a learner to complete the CBI segment covered by these objectives. Keeping the learner and teacher informed on anticipated completion time helps prevent lessons from being broken at inappropriate times. It has also been found that learners use this information as a measure of progress and achievement level. Learners who complete the segment faster than the anticipated time see it as a reward for extra effort. Those learners who take longer find the information a motivator, causing them to move faster on future units.

One danger in informing learners of anticipated completion times is that learners will not start a unit if they don't think they have enough to time to complete it. To minimize wasted time and maximize learner achievement, CBI experiences should be broken down into subunits that take no longer than 15 to 20 minutes to complete. Complex simulations which take longer to complete should provide options for saving and returning to where they left off so that a learner can stop if necessary at the end of a 15- to 20-minute block.

The objective frames may also be used to inform the learner of the title of the lesson segment that just precedes the current segment and the one that follows it. Access to lesson segments may be facilitated through some type of lesson index or menu (discussed later in this chapter), but the learner needs some orientation on his or her current status if such indexes are to be effectively utilized.

Direction frames

Direction frames provide instructions to the learner on the operation of the program. Detailed instructions should generally be in the form of printed documentation, which accompanies the program. Experience has shown that there is some danger in relying on external documentation as the sole source for such information. Printed documentation has a way of getting lost or being locked away when it is most needed. A summary of essential program operation instructions should be available as a computer-based file. Learners may not need directions each time they use the program, but access to these frames should be made optional for the user. The option for access should be provided

One Moment Please!

The computer is
selecting the test
items.

The computer is storing
information.

Please don't press the
reset key or turn the
computer off. It will
be finished in (5) sec.

Figure 5.4 "WAIT" frames

at the beginning of the program and at various points throughout the program where the information might be helpful or needed.

Direction frames should include a list of any special resources required by the lesson, i.e., reference books, a pocket calculator, additional disks, etc. It should describe prerequisites to the current unit and any special options or methods of operation that the learner should be aware of. The learner and/or teacher should be informed of any diagnostic or evaluative information which the program will maintain, and they should be told how to access this information. Nonstandard keyboard conventions and external device functions should be explained in your instructions, i.e., special key functions to access help frames, frame backup, cursor movement, light pen functions, videodisc functions, and so on.

Not all direction frames should be optional, nor should all direction frames appear at the beginning of a program. One of the most effective and useful forms of the direction frame informs the learner to WAIT while the computer or some external device is getting ready or doing some sort of task. Figure 5.4 shows the type of message that might appear on two such direction frames.

Keep instructions informal and jargon free. Messages like "loading a data file" or "booting up the videodisc player" have little meaning to the average user. Write at the level of, and use terms that are familiar to, your learner. Instead of telling the learner to press "CTRL-A," inform the learner "While holding down the key marked CONTROL, press the 'A' key." It may take a few more words, but the directions will be more understandable and useful to the learner.

Directions should be kept short and concise, including only the information the learner needs to interact with the current portion of the CBI program. Specific direction summaries, in the form of help pages, should be accessible to the learner any time the information is relevant. Directions should anticipate learner questions and should be kept as consistent as possible throughout a program or series of programs.

Except in the case of nonreaders, a teacher should not have to give instructions or directions to the users of your programs. Such information should be readily available and readable by the intended user in the form of optional instruction/direction frames.

Help frames

Help frames may serve a similar function to that of the direction frames discussed above, but they often differ greatly in the form they take. Help pages are characterized by their conciseness and general availability.

Help frames are not intended to present new material but to provide short reminders of information already presented or available in more detail someplace else. For a help frame to be of any value, it must provide the solution to an immediate need. Each help frame should be limited to providing specific help or assistance which may be required at a particular point in a program. Never present more than three help frames at a time. If the learner requires more, then the program itself needs to be revised.

The function of a particular help frame should be derived from the failure point analysis described earlier in this book, and from a careful field test and evaluation of the program before it is marketed or put to general use. Help frames may be used to provide a quick reference to nonstandard keyboard conventions or option commands which may be typed in place of a normal response. They may be used to provide the learner with short definitions of new vocabulary words or mathematical tables which they may need to look up quickly. In simulations, they are often

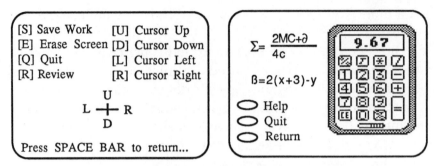

Figure 5.5   Help frames

effectively used to provide the learner access to problem-solving tools, such as a calculator or timing device, which the learner may require to solve a particular portion of the simulation. Help frames can be used to provide immediate access to almost any type of information or resource associated with the computer.

Figure 5.5 shows two different help pages. The first help page provides the learner help on the mechanics of using the computer keyboard to move the cursor, or on how to select various options available while the program is being run. The second frame provides the learner help in the form of a calculator to use, if desired, in solving a particular simulation problem. This frame also provides the formulas the learner may need. These are provided without explanation of their use or meaning. Remember, help frames are for quick reference, they should not become a lesson in themselves.

When a learner leaves a help frame or help sequence, he/she should always return to the frame they were on when they made the request for help. This is important in maintaining program continuity and in maintaining lesson orientation and frame transition. It also allows learners to use or review the information that caused them to seek help in the first place.

There are times when the help sequence is not going to be sufficient to solve the problem or to provide the necessary help. Most help pages should provide instructions on what the learner should do if more help is needed, including how to quit the program or how to review a previous portion of the program. Figure 5.5 illustrates how this was accomplished in two examples.

Not all orientation information requires a separate frame. Many times it is more effective to provide some of the orientation information discussed above as a part of dialogue or criterion frames. Whether provided in separate frames or in conjunction with other information, orientation information is critical to the effective utilization of a CBI program. It should not be ignored or left to chance.

5.3 MENU/INDEX FRAMES

Menu or index frames provide learners with a broad but brief picture of the structure of your CBI program or available program options. Their major purpose is to present learners with a number of lesson or program options and to allow the learner to select those options of interest.

Menu frames get their name because they function much as a menu in a restaurant does. You are shown the available choices and then are asked to make a selection, using a number or letter associated with it. Figure 5.6 shows a typical menu arrangement.

From the menu frame shown in Figure 5.6, the student could learn that there are five different lessons available on this program and a section titled "Problems." The menu does not tell the learner the objectives or any directions associated with any of the available units. This information appears on frames specifically designed for that purpose, which will be available once the learner selects a specific lesson.

One of the biggest problems CBI designers have when designing menu frames is trying to cram too much information onto a single screen. If you have more options than can comfortably be put on one screen, then you should group similar options under general titles which you can use on the main menu. The selection from the main menu could then lead the learner to a secondary menu which contains more specific options. Figure 5.7

Drafting: Technical Sketching

Tools and Techniques.........................1
Sketching in Three Dimensions.............2
Oblique...3
Isometric..4
Two-point/Angular Perspective.............5
Problems..6

Select the number of the lesson you
wish to take and press ENTER> ▨

Figure 5.6   Standard menu frame

Drafting
Technical Sketching: Isometric

Characteristics...................................1
Uses...2
Sketching Procedures..........................3
Problems...4
Return to Main Menu........................5

Select the lesson you wish to be begin
with and press the ENTER key > ▨

Figure 5.7   Sub-menu frame

shows a secondary menu which the student might be shown if they selected the number "4" (Isometric) from the menu shown in Figure 5.6.

Notice the title line on the secondary menu shown in Figure 5.7. It indicates that the learner is currently working on a disk or lesson titled "Drafting," is involved in a unit titled "Technical Sketching," and is currently making a selection from a module titled "Isometric." The use of titles and subtitles helps the learner understand where he/she is at in a program, and at what menu level. When designing menu/index frames, make the main index distinct from any sub-indexes, and establish a readily apparent relationship between indexes. This relationship can best be established by developing a standardized layout and by utilizing overlapping labels. The relationship can also be established on each of the related menus by providing an option that takes the learner "Back to main menu," and/or back to the next level of sub-menu.

While using sub-menus can be a way to avoid putting too much information and too many options on a single frame, you should be careful not to get the learner lost by taking him/her to too many different menu levels. It is recommended that sub-menus never be allowed to get more than two levels below the main menu.

Menu/index frames should do more than just show the learner the available options. The frame can also be used to tell the learner their current location in the lesson, the portions of the lesson they have completed, where they can go from the current sub-lesson, and how they can get there.

Lesson routing may be one of the most important functions of a menu/index frame. Designing a menu frame to look like a simple flow-chart is one effective way of showing a learner the conceptual relationship that exists between sub-lessons. Figure 5.8 shows an example of this type of menu frame.

Notice in Figure 5.8 that the levels of the flow-chart are not identical. In this lesson, learners were required to take prerequisite modules before they could select lower-level modules. In the example shown in Figure 5.8, the learner had completed the first

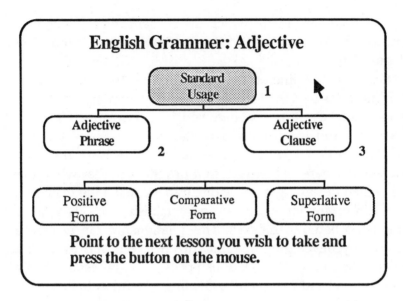

Figure 5.8   Flow-chart menu frame

module. The box enclosing the module title has been colored in by the computer to indicate successful completion. Modules 2 and 3 are currently available to the learner, or the learner may still choose to review the completed module number 1. Modules that require modules 2 and 3 as prerequisites are shown on the screen without any emphasis and without numbers associated with the options. Learners may not select these modules until the prerequisite modules have been mastered. The learner was informed that this would be the case before the menu was first shown. Even though the learner is blocked from making some selections from the menu, the menu is still helping the learner understand where the current options fit into the total lesson plan.

Marking lesson modules that the learner has completed acts both as an organizer for the learner and as a subtle reward for their effort. As modules are completed, learners see visually that they are making progress toward the completion of the total lesson or experience.

In addition to marking the units the learner has completed, it is often a good idea to mark the next unit the learner should take. Figure 5.9 shows a standard menu frame where the first two units

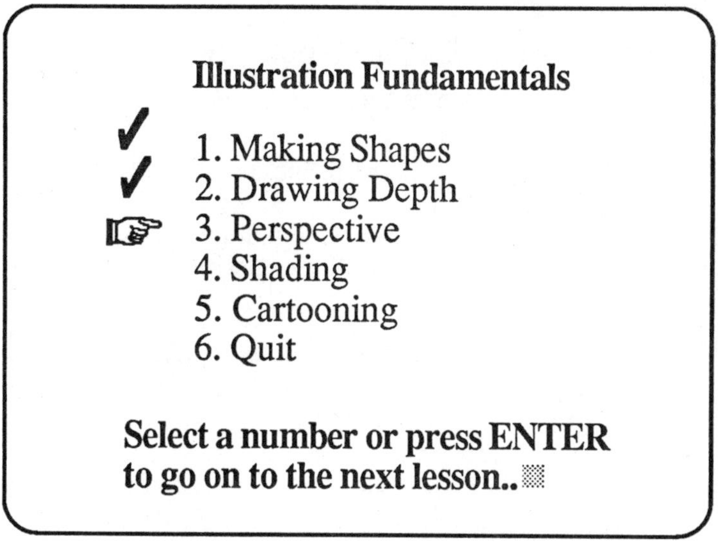

Illustration Fundamentals

✔ 1. Making Shapes
✔ 2. Drawing Depth
☞ 3. Perspective
    4. Shading
    5. Cartooning
    6. Quit

**Select a number or press ENTER
to go on to the next lesson..**

Figure 5.9   Marking menu selections

have been completed and marked with a checkmark. The third unit is marked by a pointing finger to indicate that it is the next logical unit to take. In this program the learner was not blocked from skipping around, but units were listed in the preferred order in which the learner should take them. If the learner selected a number other than the one marked with the pointing finger, the finger would move to that selection. The marking of a selection before the selection is finalized is important and useful. It provides the learner feedback they can use to double check the selection before the computer acts on it. If the learner wished to proceed with the program in the recommended sequence as indicated by the original arrow, all the learner had to do was press the return key to make the predetermined selection.

Option number 6 in Figure 5.9 is a "Quit" option. When designing menu/index frames, it is essential to provide an option for the learner to either return to a higher level menu or to quit the program from the current menu. Selection of the "Quit" option may be required by some programs to allow the computer either to close any open storage files or to store information until the next time the learner is prepared to continue the lesson. Many

Business Correspondence
Parts of a Business Letter

1. Date Line   5. Subject Line
2. Reference Line   6. Message
3. Mailing Notations   7. Signature Block
4. Inside Address   8. Postscript

Type the number of the lesson segment
you would like to review and press
ENTER.▓

Press ESC to return to the lesson..

Figure 5.10   Review menu

learners are afraid to turn off a computer unless told to do so. Even if the "Quit" option does nothing more than end the program, it does provide the learner a way out of the program without simply turning off the computer.

In all of the menu/index frames described thus far, key words have been used in the option listing. Menus should not contain long explanations of the available options. If it is felt that more explanation may be required, access to optional information frames should be provided from the menu. If additional information frames are used, they should be programmed so that they always bring the learner back to the most recent menu.

In addition to the main routing menus, menus could also be designed to aid learners in reviewing portions of a lesson. Placed at the end of a lesson, or accessible while the lesson is being presented in the form of help pages, review menus provide the learner access to individual frames or concept groupings of three or four frames. Generally, a review menu, such as the one shown in Figure 5.10, should provide the learner access to small, meaningful segments of a module or lesson which take no more than three to five minutes to complete. When a learner uses a review menu to access a portion of a program, the learner should be returned to that menu at the end of the review segment. An option should then be provided so that the learner can return to the point where the lesson was interrupted, or to some other appropriate point in the lesson. When complex branching techniques are used, as in the example just described, it is almost always advisable to backtrack through the major branching points so that learners do not lose track of where they've been and where they're going.

Lesson routing is just one of the functions menu/index style frames can serve in a CBI program. As discussed in the previous chapter, one goal of an effective CBI lesson should be to make the mechanics of the program as personal as possible. Menus have been found to be one of the best ways to make the computer react to the needs of the learner and not force the learner to figure out the needs of the computer. The menu format can be used anywhere the learner needs to make a choice between two or more responses shown on the screen. For example, menu frames may be used to present keyboard options in a help frame or as part of a series of dialogue frames. The learner, instead of having to remember a long list of abstract keyboard functions, can select from the menu the function he/she wants the computer to perform (see Figure 5.11). This type of menu can often be placed in an unobtrusive functional area of a series of dialogue frames, or it may be accessed through a designated "Help" key.

The menu approach works well when the learner is asked questions having two or more answers, such as multiple-choice questions. In simulation programs, menu responses permit the learner to try out a series of options very quickly. Figure 5.12 shows one of a series of frames from a simulation on fire safety. The learner must decide what type of extinguisher to use from this menu. Once that decision is made, and depending on what the decision is, the learner will next be presented with a new menu to determine where and/or how the extinguisher is to be applied. If the learner continues to make correct choices, the menu decision-making process continues. A wrong choice and the learner is provided a menu to determine how his/her "last will and testament" is to be divided.

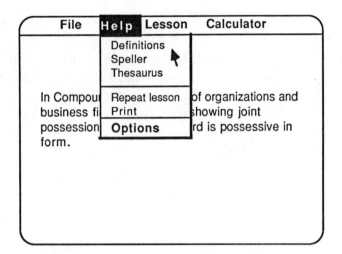

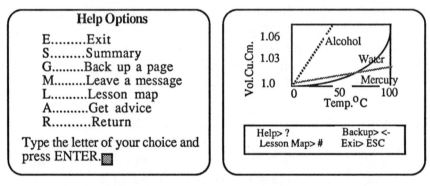

Figure 5.11   Option help menus

One unique variation of the menu frame is what might be called a picture menu. In many learning situations it is necessary for a learner to identify, locate, and/or diagnose a problem on some concrete object. Figure 5.13 shows a simulation of an electrical circuit. By pointing a light pen at critical points along the circuit, the learner is permitted to test what is occurring at that point. By performing a series of such tests, the learner must deduce where the problem lies and what action should be taken. In this particular example, a light pen was used to make the selection because it more closely simulated the actual testing procedure. Similar types of picture menus could be developed in medical CBI programs, chemical and other scientific experiments, artistic de-

You have just walked into the kitchen and a pan on the stove is in flame. What do you try to put it out with?

Water	**Dirt**	**Table Cloth**
Salt	**C O2**	**Nothing**

Type the first letter of your choice
and press ENTER.. ▓

Figure 5.12   Simulation decision menu

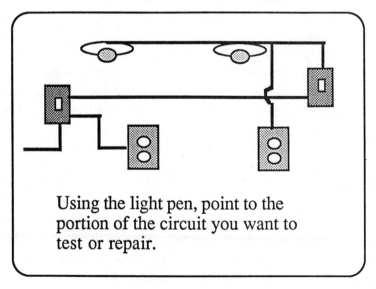

Using the light pen, point to the portion of the circuit you want to test or repair.

Figure 5.13   Picture menu

sign, equipment repair, and numerous other educational and training areas.

When designing menu frames, CBI designers should make every effort to make option selection as rapid and easy as possible. The following are a few recommendations which have been found to help this process.

Left justify options to help learner scan.   The way you organize the information on the frame has a great deal to do with how fast the learner locates the desired option. Placing option labels in a straight column lined up on the left side of the frame seems to be the most efficient way.

Learner's response should be limited to a single letter, number, or keyword.   Learners should not have to do a lot of typing to make their selection known to the computer. Asking the learner to type a single letter, number, or short keyword is generally the best way to bring this about. To eliminate almost all typing, consider using the arrow key, present on most computers, to move a marker up and down the available options until the correct one is marked. The Return/Enter key can then be used to complete the selection process. Another technique, which has been effectively used for the physically handicapped, is to allow the computer to slowly highlight one option at a time. When the correct option is highlighted, the learner can push any key on the keyboard, or some other input device, to accept the highlighted option. Devices such as light pens and touch-sensitive screens have also been used to simplify the selection process.

Require that the learner press the Return/Enter key before the option selection is accepted.   Generally, it is best to mark a selection when it is first made, allow the learner to see the selection after it has been marked or highlighted, and then force the learner to press the Return/Enter key to indicate that the marked selection is the correct one. This may seem contrary to the previous guideline, but learners who select the wrong menu option have to spend a lot of time going through an unwanted lesson, or they have to restart the entire disk. Requiring the learner to press a second key provides a check against such mistakes; and it has been found to be more efficient in the long run.

Clearly label all index/menus. The learner should always know the level of menu, and how it relates to other menus. The options should be clearly labeled. Writing good menu labels is a difficult task since they must be both concise and clear. Potential labels should be tried on a typical audience before they are finalized in the program. Sub-indexes should be labeled differently from main indexes, and the purpose of that particular index should be clear to the learner. A label like "Menu 4C" is of little help to the learner on the function or relationship of the menu.

Standardize index formats and response modes. The general format of the index/menus used in a program should remain constant throughout the program. The format should be different from that used in other frames in the program but should remain simple and motivating. Response modes should remain the same throughout the program. Avoid using optional input devices such as game paddles, light pens, etc., for option selection, unless you are sure that such devices will be present on every computer that your program will be run on. Requiring a potential user to spend thirty to one hundred dollars extra just to be able to use your program is not a good policy unless the special nature of its end use requires it.

Provide easy access in and out of the menu frame. Learners should be informed and reminded how to access any available menu frame. Once at the menu, it should be readily apparent how to get out of it, or how to move to the desired location in the program.

Place option labels in the order you would generally recommend to the learner. If there is a preferred sequence, make it evident to the learner. Even if the learner has unlimited choice of all available options, pre-marking the next option on the list is appropriate and can save a great deal of learner time.

5.4 SUMMARY

Frames are the units which make up that portion of a computer program displayed on a screen or monitor. All frames should serve a purpose, be informative, and lead to learner interaction. Simple frames are generally more effective than complex ones. They should motivate and attract attention without distracting from the main message of the frame.

Orientation frames include title frames, goal/objective frames, direction frames, and help frames. The title frame informs the user of the title of the program contained on the disk and important copyright information. Goal/objective frames tell the user the purpose or function the program is designed to fulfill. Direction frames give instructions and directions on how to operate the program and interact with the computer. Help frames provide the user with a quick reference and should be available anytime the help or reference may be applicable.

Menu/index frames show the user a listing of available options and the means for selecting the desired option. A variety of layouts can be developed, including restaurant-style menus and flow-chart menus. Marking lessons that have been completed, and recommended lessons, can help keep the learner oriented, especially where different levels of sub-menus are used.

5.5 ISSUES AND ACTIVITIES

1. Design a title page for a program you are thinking of developing. Ask a few friends if they can tell from the title page what the program is about, and ask them if they would be attracted to your program if they saw that title page on the screen. If you used color in your design, think how it would look on a black and white screen.
2. List all the options you would include in a program and then design a series of quick reference help pages that

describe each option with a symbol, or three words or less. See if a friend understands the help page. Redesign it to meet any suggested changes.

3. Find a CBI program that comes with a set of printed instructions. Rewrite the instructions as computer frames. Remember the limits of the computer screen (40 letters wide by 24 lines long). The instructions shouldn't be longer or require more than six screens.

4. Find a computer disk with six or more programs on it and design a menu frame for that disk.

5. Make a flow-chart style menu for this book. Are there some chapters that are prerequisite to other chapters? The menu should reflect the organization options you would provide the learner if the book were available only on a computer.

5.6 REFERENCES

Burke, R. L. *CBI Sourcebook*. Englewood Cliffs, NJ: Prentice-Hall, 1982.

Fleming, M., & Levie, H. *Instructional Message Design: Principles from the Behavioral Sciences*. Englewood Cliffs, NJ: Educational Technology Publications, 1978.

Heines, J. M. *Screen Design: Strategies for Computer-Assisted Instruction*. Bedford, MA: Digital Equipment Corp., 1984.

Hofmeister, A. *Microcomputer Applications in the Classroom*. New York: Holt, Rinehart & Winston, 1984.

Kamins, S., & Waite, M. *Apple Backpack: Humanized Programming in BASIC*. Peterborough, NH: BYTE/McGraw-Hill, 1982.

Markle, S. M. *Good Frames and Bad: A Grammar of Frame Writing*. New York: John Wiley & Sons, 1969.

Merrill, M. D., & Tennyson, R. D. *Teaching Concepts: An Instructional Design Guide*. Englewood Cliffs, NJ: Educational Technology Publications, 1977.

Meyers, J., & Tognazzini, B. *Design Guidelines*. Cupertino, CA: Apple Computer, 1982.

Minnesota Educational Computing Consortium. *Designing Instructional Computing Materials*. St. Paul, MN: Author, 1982.

6

Designing Instructional Frames

6.0 INTRODUCTION

In the previous chapter we discussed the design of management frames. The main purpose of these frames is to guide the learner through the instructional experience, providing directions and help along the way. While these CBI frames are important in the instructional process, they do not teach. In this chapter we discuss the design of the two major types of frames that do. Dialogue frames present information to the learner, as well as carry out an interactive dialogue/feedback between the learner and the computer. Criterion frames assess learning performance and provide feedback on results and follow-up activities.

As the CBI designer, you are the real teacher. You are the one who communicates with the learner. The computer and the individual instructional frames are the essential go-between. They take the design you put into them and transmit that information to the learner. In designing instructional frames, always keep in mind the importance of your role in the instructional process. The computer is simply an extension to you. If you design poor instruction, the computer will convey poor instruction.

The content of instructional frames should reflect the goals and objectives discussed in earlier chapters. Their design should be a synthesis, a combination, of all the areas of planning you have already done and should reflect the needs, interests, and abilities of the learner. Messages should be written in a language the learner understands, and examples taken from the learner's own background. The instructional sequence itself should begin where the previous learning left off. Instructional analysis and audience analysis are not just "make-work" projects. They are essential to your ability to design effective instructional frames. And the goals and objectives you established are the framework upon which you build them.

Instructional frame design is an art, and you are the architect. The tools and experience of others will help you get started; but it is your own creativity and your experience as a communicator and master teacher that will determine—in the end—how successful you are as a designer of CBI instructional frames.

6.1 DIALOGUE FRAMES

Teaching frames are referred to by many names. This author chooses to use the term "dialogue frames," borrowed from Alfred Bork. Bork (1980) defined "dialog" as "a 'conversation' between a student and a teacher, where the student is at a computer display and the teacher is conducting the dialog through the medium of a computer program." The definition seems to fit perfectly. It reflects the function of a dialogue frame in a CBI program. A dialogue is a two-way interactive communication. We refer throughout this section to dialogue frames as if all parts of the dialogue appear on a single display. More often than not, however, a dialogue frame is really a series of frames consisting of from two to five individual displays. When everyone tries to talk at once, the result is confusion, not dialogue. The same thing happens with computers. The various functional roles must be played out in sequence if the dialogue is to be meaningful.

Programmers decide the sequence a dialogue should take.

Over the years numerous models have been suggested. In this section we discuss two approaches, one in which the rule precedes the examples, and the other in which the opposite is true. There is some disagreement among professionals on which is best. I feel that both have merit in certain situations. Your responsibility is to understand the strengths and weaknesses of each and to be prepared to apply—or adapt—each to the appropriate CBI environment.

RULEG approach

One of the most popular strategies for sequencing an instructional dialogue is the RULEG system. It was first suggested by J. L. Evans, R. Glaser, and L. E. Homme, and it gets its name from the order in which the rules (RULE) and examples (EG) are presented. The first part of a RULEG dialogue frame, or sequence of frames, presented is the rule, which the learner is expected to apply. Recall the learning objectives and task analysis you developed earlier. From them you should be able to develop a series of rules—definitions, formulas, concepts, principles, empirical laws, cause-effect relationships, etc., which, when taught, will cause the learner to perform or behave in a certain way. This performance or behavior is your learning objective. The following are examples of rules:

A simple sentence is a complete grammatical unit having one subject and one predicate, either or both of which may be compound.

common law. a. The general and ordinary law of a country or community. **b.** The unwritten law that receives its binding force from immemorial usage and universal reception.

$A = 4\Box r^2$ (Area of a sphere)

Color contrast appears greatest along the border between the light and dark areas of an image.

When a Type (T:) instruction is modified by the Hang (TH:) modifier, the cursor remains at the first character position following the displayed text, rather than advancing to the next line.

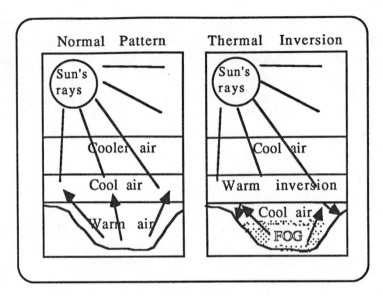

Figure 6.1   Rule dialogue frame

A rule in a CBI frame need not be limited to cold, hard facts. It can be dressed up in ways that make it more interesting and therefore easier to remember. Figure 6.1 shows a rule on the effects of a warm air inversion. It is presented in visual rather than verbal form.

The preparation of the rule portion of a dialogue frame or series of frames is not as easy as it sounds. The rule must be concise, but it must also be comprehensive, containing enough information to allow learners to discriminate between ideas, objects, and skills that meet the rule and those that do not. It should be evident to the learners, as they analyze the rule, just what its criterial attributes are. Learners can then respond appropriately, that is, separate the responses that correctly match the rule from those that do not. In the example shown in Figure 6.1, one criterial attribute for a thermal inversion is a warm layer of air trapped between two colder layers of air. This situation is a necessary condition for a thermal inversion. It is reinforced by the contrasting condition of a normal pattern. Many dictionary and textbook definitions list insufficient criterial attributes and so do not meet the requirements of a good rule. The dictionary, for example,

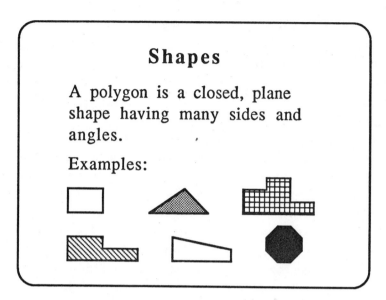

Figure 6.2 Rule with positive examples

defines "cedar" as "Any of a large number of coniferous trees having fragrant durable wood." Since there are thousands of coniferous trees in the world, many having fragrant and durable wood, which are not cedars, it would be extremely difficult for a learner to develop discrimination learning based on the criterial attributes given. A rule, to be effective, must contain a sufficient amount of detail to permit the learner to discriminate members from nonmembers of a concept.

The second part of the RULEG approach is the presentation of examples. "Examples" should include both positive examples (those that match the rule) and non-examples (those that look similar, but fail to meet all the criteria). Figure 6.2 shows a frame containing both a rule and a series of positive examples.

The selection of examples, like the wording of a rule, is very important. If all of the examples shown in Figure 6.2 had four sides, the learner might think that a polygon must have four sides (that four-sidedness is a criterial attribute of the rule), even though the rule does not suggest this. If all the filled-in shapes were clear, the learner might think the word "plane" implies "plain in color."

If you were to prepare a list of irregular verbs, and you only included the words beat, blow, begin, break, and burst, you might lead the learner into believing that all irregular verbs begin with B. Use a wide variety of examples, all of which meet the criterial attributes of the rule. Include only enough common, non-criterial attributes to make your point.

In addition to examples that meet the attributes of the rule, items that are sometimes called "non-examples" should be used. Where examples were positive instances, non-examples are negative instances, that is, instances of objects or ideas that do not meet the established rule. Selecting non-examples sounds simple, but it really isn't. Non-examples are included in the dialogue frame to further reinforce the criterial attributes that permit discrimination learning. Suppose you select a cow as a non-example of a butterfly. The learner certainly could discriminate between the cow and the butterfly, but few people get cows and butterflies mixed up in the first place. A better non-example would be a hummingbird. A hummingbird has many things in common with a butterfly, but each differ on one or more of the criterial attributes of the rule that make a butterfly a butterfly.

The scope of this book does not permit me to discuss all the criteria for selecting examples and non-examples. I recommend that CBI designers read more on this topic. One excellent source is a book entitled *Teaching Concepts: An Instructional Design Guide* by Merrill and Tennyson (1977). Selection is only part of the problem, though. CBI designers must know how to place examples and non-examples on a frame or a series of frames in such a way as to permit the learner to make comparisons. One way is to pair examples and non-examples on a single frame (see Figure 6.3). If that is not possible, CBI designers should provide some mechanism for the learner to move about between related frames. Arrow keys, available on most computer keyboards, do this very effectively. The fact that an arrow signifies direction helps the learner remember its function in a program, and the proximity of the arrows to one another on the keyboard makes it possible for the learner to move quickly from one display to the next, according to the direction signified by the arrow. In a visual display, com-

PRONOUNS: Nominative forms
The subject of a verb should be in the nominative case.

Wrong	Her and me are classmates.
Right	She and I are classmates.
Wrong	Neither Bob nor him had the answer.
Right	Neither Bob nor he had the answer.

Press the SPACE BAR to continue...

Figure 6.3   Paired example/non-example frame

parisons can be made through an animated sequence. Suppose, for example, you want to teach someone how to hold a tennis racket. You could design an animated sequence that shows the hand moving from the incorrect position to the correct position. The animation could then be placed under learner control, perhaps through the use of game paddles. The learner can move the animation forward and backward with time enough to study the details of the two extreme hand positions as well as those of the lesser positions in between.

EGRUL approach

The EGRUL approach differs in the sequence in which the examples and rules are presented to the learner. Many learning theorists believe learners should see a number of examples before the concept or rule is presented. Learners then have a context in which to fit the rule, and the rule will have more meaning and will be learned faster and remembered longer. Discovery learning applies many of the EGRUL principles, since both are inductive.

Both approaches are useful in particular learning situations. It is up to you, the CBI designer, to determine which is most appropriate.

Interaction

We have talked about the first two parts of the dialogue frame, the rule and the examples. The third part is the practice, or interaction, function. While not specifically stated, it is used in both the RULEG and EGRUL approaches. You should, of course, select interaction techniques that are appropriate to the desired learning outcome. You should utilize as wide a variety of appropriate interactions, not just those that require pure recall and memorization of basic information. The major goal is to take even very young learners beyond the basic information—to help them extend and generalize to new examples and new problems. The purpose of CBI interaction design is not just to see if the learner can get the correct answer, but to see if the learner understands and can apply the principle, process, or concept being taught.

Open interactive dialogue. Consider the type of interaction. The frames we have been discussing in the last few pages are grouped into a functional category we call dialogue frames. When we carry out a dialogue with someone, questions can be asked and answered. There is currently a movement toward using more open ended dialogues in computer systems. Recent developments in artificial intelligence and in what are being called "expert systems" are opening new doors for CBI designers. General application of these new techniques may still be in the future for you, but there are some things you can do now to improve the open interactive dialogue capabilities of your program.

One easy way to encourage open dialogue is to provide the learner with an opportunity to leave a short comment or inquiry message for the instructor. The message can be stored on a disk until the instructor has time to read the message and provide either a computer based or a personal response to the learner. Dialogue frames should notify learners of the availability of this option. Where appropriate, they should also provide an easy

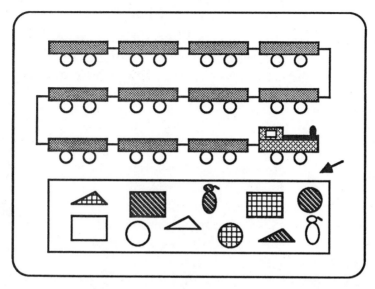

Figure 6.4 Dialogue inquiry

mechanism, perhaps a help frame, for learners to leave messages without interfering with the general flow of the program.

Inquiry dialogue. Dialogue frames can also be designed to permit learners to ask what might be called "What if?" questions. Simulation programs make general use of this inquiry design; but it may be applied to other types of CBI programs as well. Figure 6.4 illustrates a dialogue frame in which the learner is asked to experiment with shapes and colors to determine "what if" the colors and shapes are placed in different sequences. In the first application, the learner uses a joystick or mouse to point the arrow at objects and move them into the train cars. The order of the objects on the train cars must match a predefined rule, but there are numerous combinations that will suffice. If the learner places an object in a car so that the order doesn't fit the rule, the car simply dumps the object out. The purpose of the dialogue is to allow the learner to discover and generalize a concept rule so that he/she can load the train repeatedly without making a single mistake. This same dialogue frame is used to allow learners to formulate their own rules, which the computer tries to solve in the same fashion. In this instance the interaction between learner and computer is truely give and take. Dialogue frames provide optional and remedial rules and examples to learners who need additional help in interacting before they move on to the criterion frames.

Feedback

The final, but by no means least important, function of the dialogue frame is the feedback function. A great deal of research has gone into the type and frequency of the feedback that should be provided to learners. Much depends on the nature of the content and the ability of the learner to process information. Even so, there are some guidelines that generally should be applied in any situation. First, learners need to know when their response is correct or incorrect. They need to know about their progress if any improvement is to take place.

A learner may choose not to enter into the dialogue. Instead of responding when expected to do so, he or she presses the Return/Enter key without typing any other response. In this situation the learner should not be provided with the correct answer. Dialogue feedback is only useful when the learner actively participates in the exchange. Generally, a learner should not be provided with a means of finding the correct answer until an attempt at response has been made. Answer sheets should be kept out of the hands of learners. Be sure your help frames don't give too much help, or the wrong kind of help, to the learner.

Feedback should occur as closely as possible to the response, whether correct or incorrect. Learners need to know that the feedback is a direct consequence of their response. Simple feedback is effective if it immediately follows the response; but it must also be apparent that a relationship exists between the act and the consequence. Variation in the type of feedback will establish this relationship. Even when learners get all the answers correct, they need to know that the feedback is in some way tailored to and appropriate to their response. This is especially true for correct versus incorrect answers. Make feedback to a correct response more motivating than feedback to an incorrect response. Feedback that is equally exciting and motivating no matter what the response loses its value. Some programs unfortunately make feedback to an incorrect response more exciting than that to a correct response. The learner quickly discovers how much more fun it is to respond incorrectly and does so for the rest of the program.

Some researchers and designers feel that positive feedback should occur only for correct responses. Feedback for incorrect responses should be negative. I think *all* feedback should be positive to reinforce learning. Feedback to a correct response should reward and motivate learners to continue to do their best. It should contain design elements that make it more exciting and worthwhile for them to strive to achieve the correct response.

Feedback to an incorrect response should be relatively neutral. Still, it should provide information that will help the learner do better the next time. Learners should first be rewarded for their effort and then shown how to focus and direct it.

Whenever possible, feedback to an incorrect response should attempt to assess the reason why the learner made the incorrect response, and it should be tailored to help overcome the problem. Figure 6.5 shows a frame with positive feedback to an "incorrect" response. The learner missed the response only by misspelling the word. Notice that the feedback doesn't tell the learner that he/she was wrong. That might undo any valuable learning that had occurred. Instead, the learner is told that the answer is correct but the spelling needs improvement.

The frequency of both interaction and feedback should be based on two factors: the newness, or unfamiliarity, of the material; and the meaningfulness or ability of the information to fit into a pre-established set of competencies. Information that must be memorized out of any applied context requires more interaction and feedback. This suggests that all interaction and feedback, whether in tutorial, drill-and-practice, or simulation CBI, should occur in some contextual environment where possible.

Dialogue frames may involve a simple series of three or four frames or a complex series of branching activities. No matter how complex or simple the dialogue series is, you should always strive

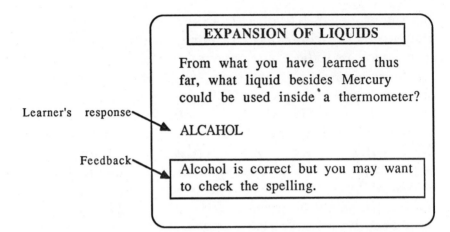

Learner's response

Feedback

Figure 6.5   Dialogue frame with feedback

to improve the interactive, conversational quality of the dialogue. Whether you are designing a drill-and-practice, simulation, or tutorial-style CBI program, it is the quality of the dialogue frames that is going to make or break your program.

6.2 CRITERION FRAMES

Criterion frames, though similar in appearance to some practice dialogue frames, serve a very different function in the overall CBI lesson plan. Essentially a test/evaluation frame, a criterion frame is designed to assess a learner's progress and readiness to move forward in the lesson. A learner's progress is assessed against a predefined set of criteria, not against that of other learners. The development of criterion frames should directly reflect the CBI objectives you established in the beginning, with the criterion items and accompanying interaction designed to test the desired learning behavior outcome.

Most criterion frames come in two parts, the criterion test item and the response feedback. For a criterion test item to be effective, it must separate the learners who have met the preset learning objective from those who have not. While this sounds easy, CBI designers seem to have a great deal of trouble with it. Failure apparently comes from two sources. Sometimes designers fail to use pre-established objectives as their guide when preparing criterion items. Criterion items should be based on program objectives, not specific content. During field testing, determine if there is a problem with your program's ability to teach learners to meet objectives. If necessary, make changes. If the objectives suggest more than one learning behavior outcome, it may be necessary for you to include more than one criterion item for that objective.

Another source of failure is that designers, even when considering their learning objectives, often fail to require the kind of learning behavior that is specified in the objectives. They use multiple-choice questions when they are supposed to be testing problem-solving or psychomotor skills, for example. Unfortunately, the computer can only judge certain types of responses. For this reason, in the rest of this section I focus on three types of criterion items that a computer can accept and judge.

Constructed response items

Constructed response items are generally the most effective in forcing learners to think and apply general rules, but they are also the most difficult to develop and judge using a computer. As implied, in a constructed response learners must construct, or create, a response. Few, if any, prompts or clues are provided by the computer, beyond the initial question or problem. The simplest form of a constructed response may be the so-called fill-in-the-blank question. Figure 6.4 is an example of a constructed response. The learner is required to place objects in train cars by following certain rules, but with many variations possible.

If the computer is to judge responses for correctness, it must be programmed with every possible correct response, or with some rule or set of rules by which it can judge the response. Where multiple answers are possible, it is difficult for the designer to anticipate all of the possible combinations. Take a simple question like "Do you want to continue with this program?" The obvious possible responses are "yes" and "no." But what about the learner who responds with a simple "Y" or with "I certainly do," "Yep," or "I think so"? You might think, "If he can't read my mind then he gets it wrong," but is this really fair? Most problems with this type of question are usually the result of poor writing. The thing you must do is to sufficiently restrict the answer options. Learn to write the questions in such a way that you can anticipate 90 percent of the possible answers.

Some programming languages handle constructed response items better than others. PILOT, for example, permits the computer to scan a portion of a student's response for a specific combination of letters. Telling the computer to watch for the letter "Y" as the first letter in the word would be a way of handling a lot of possible constructed responses on a simple yes/no item.

Sometimes constructed response items can only be judged by a live instructor, for example, essay-type responses. This doesn't mean that you shouldn't include such items in a competency frame; however, it will be necessary to record the response on the disk so that the instructor can correct it at a later time.

When designing constructed response frames, consider a few layout techniques. If the constructed response is a fill-in-the-blank item, move the cursor to the blank before the learner types in the response, and make sure you leave enough space for the longest anticipated response. The amount of blank space can prompt the learner as to the type and size of the response you are looking for. Another effective form of constructed response is the sentence completion format. Figure 6.6 illustrates both a fill-in-the-blank and a sentence completion format. The sentence completion format is usually easier to program, since the cursor does not have to be relocated within previously typed text.

Not all constructed responses need be in text form. Figure 6.6 illustrates one in which the learner moves the symbol of the sun until it matches the shadows on the illustrated box. The learner can move the sun anyplace on the screen. The computer evaluates the response by showing the learner a second box illustrating the proper shadowing from the new position. Constructed responses built around math problems often present a special format consideration. In another ex-

A large hydroelectric power plant, such as the Grand Coulee Dam can produce as much as ▦_____megawatts of electricity.

Type your response and press ENTER.

A CLONE is an organism that has been produced from a genetically
▦

Complete the sentence and press ENTER.

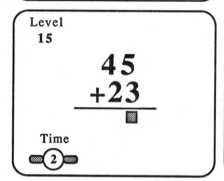

Level
15

45
+23
—————
▦

Time
◦◦(2)◦◦

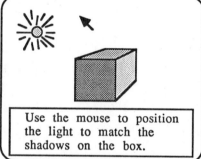

Use the mouse to position the light to match the shadows on the box.

Figure 6.6   Constructed response frames

ample from Figure 6.6 the input must be typed from right to left in order to conform to the standard technique used.

Matching response items

Matching response items consist of two sets of items which the learner is required to match up in some way. Figure 6.7 shows a typical matching response frame. It is important to select items that do not have overlapping relationships. When an item can be matched with two or more items in the opposite column, the test becomes a guessing game.

Although the design of matching response items is relatively simple, learners occasionally have problems when the response mechanism is hard to operate and understand. Generally, learners should be allowed to select an item from either column. This

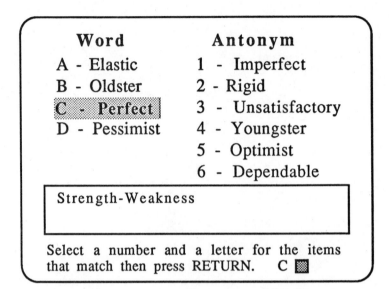

Figure 6.7 Matching response frame

means that each column must have its own unique set of labels, e.g., letters of the alphabet for one and numbers for the other. After a learner has selected an item it should be highlighted in some way. Learners need to be sure which item they are working on. When items have been correctly matched, it is a good idea to remove the matched items from the list. Move them to some other part of the screen so that the learner may review them. It is not generally good design practice to require learners to go from the first item on the list to the last in a predefined order.

One interesting variation of the matching response frame shown in Figure 6.7 is a series of programs collectively called "Arcademics" by Developmental Learning Materials. In many of these programs, learners are shown a general match item such as "verb"; then they are shown a list of words one at a time. The learner must decide if a match exists before the word disappears. The general match item changes every few seconds, and the learner must immediately adapt to the new match sequence. This gaming approach is highly motivating and allows the use of items where multiple matches are possible and desirable. In Figure 6.8,

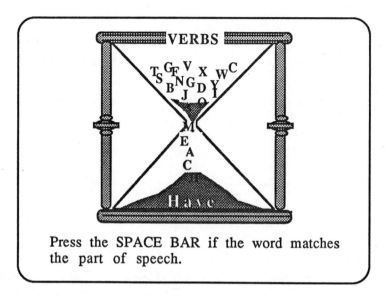

Figure 6.8   Multiple-match response frame

a part of speech is shown at the top of the hourglass, and a series of possible word matches are generated at the bottom. By pressing the space bar, the learner indicates whether a match exists or not. The part of speech then changes as words continue to appear. The learner discovers that while some words don't match some parts of speech, they may match others. It is also possible for a word to match more than one part of speech.

Multiple-choice response items

Multiple-choice response frames include criterion items for which learners select the correct answer from two or more choices. This includes the two-way response (e.g., true–false, yes–no) as well as the traditional multiple-choice response.

Response to a multiple-choice frame should be as simple as possible, usually a single letter or number. The available choices, and the method of selecting a choice should be made clear to learners. Figure 6.9 shows two typical multiple-choice and two-way response frames. If a question allows or requires more than one choice, each selection should be typed in individually followed by the Return/Enter key

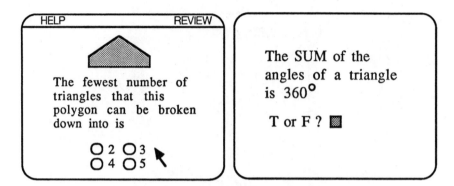

Figure 6.9   Multiple-choice response frames

being pressed. Even though a single letter/number is all that is required, learners should still press the Return/Enter key before the answer will be accepted by the computer. This gives the learner time to rethink and, if necessary, correct, the response.

Dialogue and criterion frames should not all look alike. As suggested in Chapter 1, the modern computer has many capabilities which the printed page doesn't allow. Frame design should make use of these new capabilities.

Frames should be kept simple but motivating. Test materials should be written in clear proper English. Information should be accurate, and interaction should be appropriate to the objectives the program was designed to meet. Required responses should be kept short, should be relevant, and should add to the learner's understanding. Individual frames should be evaluated in the context of the entire program so that the learner proceeds rapidly and naturally from frame to frame. These are just some of the challenges faced by the CBI frame designer.

6.3 SUMMARY

Instructional frames can be broken down into two major categories: dialogue frames and criterion frames.

Dialogue frames carry out a two-way instructional "conversation" with the learner. They are used to present information, provide examples, and interact with and respond to the learner. Basically, they are the teaching frames.

Two popular approaches to designing dialogue frames are RULEG and EGRUL. The RULEG approach begins with a rule or general description of the information being presented. The rule is followed by a series of examples, which in turn are followed by a practice session. The EGRUL approach contains all of the same elements but begins the presentation with the set of examples. These are then related together by a rule or a description, followed by learner interaction and practice.

The methods available for presenting rules, examples, and practice are limited only by the imagination of the CBI developer. Graphic, sound, animation, and text are just some of the elements that can be used to attract a learner's attention and to make the presentation and practice sessions interesting and effective.

Dialogue frames should encourage the active participation of the learner. Learner responses should be meaningful and should be used by the computer to control future dialogue frames.

Experimentation is an important element of the dialogue process. The computer can be used to support the learner's inquiries, in addition to presenting information and practice problems.

Criterion frames are essentially test/evaluation frames designed to assess learner performance. The design of criterion frames should match the performance behaviors identified with individual learning objectives. Criterion items can range from true–false style questions to performance simulations that make use of peripheral devices such as flight simulators. Criterion items generally fall into one of three categories: constructed, matching, and multiple-choice response.

Constructed response items are the most difficult for a computer to handle. Generally, however, they are the most effective in assessing higher-level performance objectives. Match items are most effective when an exact item match is to be identified, i.e., states and their capitals. Multiple-choice items present two or more choices from which learners may select a response.

6.4 ISSUES AND ACTIVITIES

1. Pick a short topic that you would like to teach someone. Teach it in a one-on-one environment and use a tape recorder to make a record of the entire event. Outline all of the activities performed by you. List specifically all of the questions that you asked, or that were asked by the learner. Try teaching the same topic to another learner, but this time limit yourself to exactly the same information and responses used in the first try. Make a record each time you have to modify your approach. Consider teaching several hundred learners the same topic. How are you going to design a dialogue that can handle all of the individual differences and questions?
2. Design a RULEG sequence to teach someone how to boil an egg.
3. Design an EGRUL sequence to teach someone what a pronoun is.
4. Design a criterion frame that tests to see if a learner can convert yards to meters. Turn the criterion frame into a game that would interest a young child.
5. Design an arcademics–type multiple-match frame to provide testing on a math skill.

6.5 REFERENCES

Bork, A. Preparing student computer dialogs: Advice to teachers. In R. P. Taylor, *The Computer in the School: Tutor, Tool, Tutee*. New York: Teachers College Press, 1980.

Burke, R. L. *CAI Sourcebook*. Englewood Cliffs, NJ: Prentice-Hall, 1982.

Fleming, M., & Levie, H. *Instructional Message Design: Principles from the Behavioral Sciences*. Englewood Cliffs, NJ: Educational Technology Publications, 1978.

Heines, J. M. *Screen Design: Strategies for Computer-Assisted Instruction*. Bedford, MA: Digital Equipment Corp., 1984.

Hofmeister, A. *Microcomputer Applications in the Classroom*. New York: Holt, Rinehart & Winston, 1984.

Kamins, S., & Waite, M. *Apple Backpack: Humanized Programming in BASIC*. Peterborough, NH: BYTE/McGraw-Hill, 1982.

Markle, S. M. *Good Frames and Bad: A Grammar of Frame Writing*. New York: John Wiley & Sons, 1969.

Merrill, M. D., & Tennyson, R. D. *Teaching Concepts: An Instructional Design Guide*. Englewood Cliffs, NJ: Educational Technology Publications, 1977.

Meyers, J., & Tognazzini, B. *Design Guidelines*. Cupertino, CA: Apple Computer, 1982.

Minnesota Educational Computing Consortium. *Designing Instructional Computing Materials*. St. Paul, MN: Author, 1982.

7

Designing Screen Displays

7.0 INTRODUCTION

To this point, the concern has been with helping you develop the content of a CBI program and with the treatment of that content in the form of program frames. This chapter and the next discuss the major screen elements that make up a computer video display and how to control and utilize each element. They will not cover the technical processes used to generate a video display; but rather will discuss in a practical manner the design techniques that you, as a CBI author, should use to present your intended content more effectively and to make your programs more interesting and motivating for the learner.

The effective design of a computer video display requires that the designer know communication and learning theory, human engineering, instructional message design, have an artistic sense of color, layout, and balance, and be cognizant of the affective emotional impact of visual images on people. Many computer based video displays have characteristics different from those generated by standard broadcast television. It is essential, therefore, that the CBI designer be sensitive to those differences, recognizing both their advantages and their limitations.

It is impossible for these two chapters alone to give you all of the ideas and information you need to design effective screens. You already possess many of the required skills, but don't realize how they relate. Other skills can be learned by your reading or attending special courses in fields related to the areas discussed above. But, in the opinion of this author, there is no substitute for experience. You will find with each CBI program you write that your intuition will get better, especially if you take the time to test your programs out and to observe carefully the impact of various screen formats. In addition to evaluating your own programs, look critically at other computer programs, especially those rated high by other people. Your interests, likes, and dislikes are not as unique as you might believe. If a program or an individual frame attracts your attention, for either positive or negative reasons, take the time to analyze it. What did the author do to make it such a good (or bad) program?

Why should you go to so much trouble to design display screens? Wasn't it enough that you had to work so hard on the program and individual frame content? The answer may be found in asking yourself why you watch a particular TV news show, or why you shop at a particular store, rather than one that may be closer or more convenient. The content, in both cases, is similar, but you probably are motivated by the way that content is presented. A well-designed CBI display will attract and motivate a learner to pay attention to the important content that you selected, as well as help the computer convey the essential information. Careful screen design, as you will see, can also be used to make your content easier to read and understand, and easier to organize and remember.

7.1 COMPUTER VIDEO SCREENS

Because many computer systems are connected to home-style television sets, many people assume that a computer-generated video display has the same capabilities as a standard television. While there

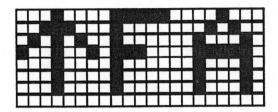

Figure 7.1   Display dot patterns

are many similarities, only the most sophisticated and expensive computers come close to the imaging capabilities of standard television.

Moreover, many computers generate screens that look very similar to a printed page, and so we are sometimes led to assume that the computer display is just a "soft," non-tangible print medium. Again, such an assumption is partly true, but there are some differences which are critical to the CBI display designer.

How does the computer form an image on the screen? If you were to take a magnifying glass and hold it up to the screen, you would discover that the letters that you see are really just groupings of dots or, as they are sometimes called, "pixels." To form different letters or graphic images, the computer simply turns on or off some of the dots or pixels. Figure 7.1 illustrates how this works.

Not all computers are capable of generating the same number of dots across or up and down a screen. The ability of the computer to control screen dots is usually referred to as its "resolution capacity." An American standard television has the ability to generate a resolution capacity of 525 rows of dots, while most computer systems have a resolution capacity of between 127 and 256 rows of dots. As a result of this lower resolution capacity, computer displays often appear coarse when compared to standard television. Curved lines that go off at an angle generally appear jagged or staircased, as shown in Figure 7.2 on page 167.

Most computer-generated displays are limited in their capacity to produce color. When you watch a standard color program on television, you see hundreds of shades and values of color. A typical computer display, on the other hand, has the capacity to produce 12 or less pure color values. Such limitations must be considered by the CBI designer, especially when color illustration materials are to be included in a frame.

Recent advances in technology, as can be seen in such computers as the Apple Macintosh and Commodor Amiga, holds promise for eliminating many of the limitations discussed above. But until such computers gain wide acceptance by the educational community, instructional designers will have to continue to design around many of the limitations of the older technology.

Like a standard television display, but unlike most printed pages, the computer video display is dynamic. Portions of the screen can be made independent of, and can be changed without affecting, other portions. This means that text or illustrative materials can remain on the screen from one frame to the next. Also, complex illustrative materials can be built, or added to, a piece at a time. Information materials that learners need from frame to frame remain, while new questions or information can be provided and constantly change in other areas of the screen. All of this, of course, requires careful planning if the screen is not to become a three ring circus.

7.2 GENERAL DISPLAY FORMATTING

As the use of computer based instructional materials continues to increase, so will the amount of time students spend looking at computer-generated video displays. Much of the research, and many of the concerns which have gone into the design of effective printed and illustrated instructional materials, should be carried over to the design of computer video displays.

Before deciding on the general format of frames, CBI designers should first know something about the capabilities of the computer they are designing for. What type of displays can it generate? Can it display both text and illustrative materials? How detailed can the graphics be? Can it generate color? How much

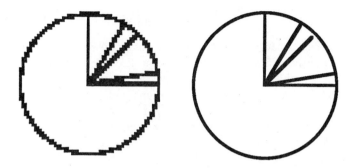

Figure 7.2   High vs low resolution "staircasing"

memory is available for various applications? How many characters can the computer display vertically and horizontally across
the screen?

With recent attempts to make computer programs transportable between various computer systems, there has been a tendency to design computer displays to the "lowest common de-
nominator," that is, to the capabilities of the least capable computer. Such a trend is counterproductive to the effective
application of computers in the instructional market.

Screen display size is usually thought of in terms of the number of characters (letters and/or numbers) a particular computer
can generate across and down the screen. The standard screen
display is either 40 or 80 character columns across and 24 character
rows down. Many modern microcomputers can shift between
these two standards as the designer dictates. Care should be taken
in using an 80 character screen if the type of monitor or television
is not known. Most inexpensive computer color monitors and
television sets are not capable of handling an 80 character image
clearly. The result is a screen display that is impossible to read.
In situations where high-resolution monochromatic monitors
(black and white, green or orange) are consistently used, the 80
column screen may be the preferred option. While the 40 column
screen is a little narrow for many applications, it is still the best
choice on most current microcomputer systems.

WORKING MODELS

These models are designed to show how things function. The model may be a life-like replica of an object such as an engine or a spinning wheel, or it may be a simulation model used in visualizing concepts not related to any actual object. One effective working model has been the stream table. This simple model can be used effectively to demonstrate stream development and soil conservation concepts. Other working models make use of color-coded parts to illustrate wiring procedures or mechanical operations. Examples of working models include model airplanes, weather instruments, and types of engines.

Figure 7.3   Packed video display

The use of the 40 column screen does place some major limits on the quantity of information that can be presented. This limit causes some designers to try to pack the screen, filling all available space with information. Figure 7.3 is an example of such a packed display. It only contains a single paragraph of information, but it appears overwhelming, unmotivating, and unreadable to the average learner. CBI designers need to learn to write more concisely and to use multiple screens or frames when large quantities of information need to be presented. Figure 7.4 illustrates how a portion of the previous frame could be made to look. The addition of an illustration makes the entire frame appear more interesting, and the use of "white space," or empty screen space, makes the information much less overwhelming. If the rest of the information in Figure 7.3 is essential, then separate frames should be designed to provide this information. Where large amounts of text are required, it may be best to provide an accompanying printed workbook.

One thing to keep in mind when designing computer video

Working Models

These models are designed to show how things function.

One effective working model is the STREAM TABLE.

This simple model can be made from grassy sod and sand and can be used to demonstrate stream development and soil conservation.

Press the SPACE BAR to continue...

Figure 7.4   Open frame display

One thing to keep in mind when designing computer video screens is that screen space is cheap. Unlike the printed page, where each page you add to a book makes each copy of the book cost more, additional video screens add very little to the cost of a program. Long text information should be broken up into short messages which can be presented successively, with the presentation rate under learner control.

In addition, video screens, or portions of video screens, can and often should be reused. If the author of the frame shown in Figure 7.4 wished to teach the learner how to build a stream table, he/she could have reused the illustrations included on this frame without having to redraw or reprogram them. As discussed earlier, video screens are dynamic. Portions of the screen can be erased and written on without affecting the remaining portions of the screen. Text and graphic portions of most screens can be separated in programming so that each can be used in future frames independently. For example, it may be desirable to reuse

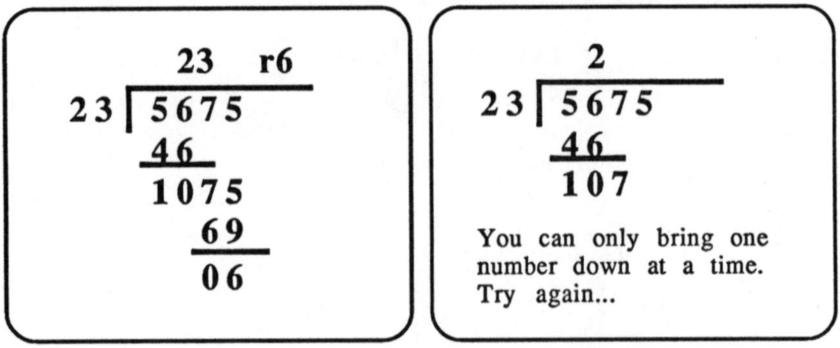

```
        23   r6
   23 | 5675
        46
        1075
          69
          06
```

```
          2
   23 | 5675
        46
        107
```
You can only bring one
number down at a time.
Try again...

Figure 7.5   Selectivity erasing displays

an illustration without the accompanying text in a criterion frame on the concept.

Utilizing the dynamic capabilities of the computer video screen can be one of the most effective and motivating things you can do in screen design. Not only can you reveal and reuse different parts of the screen at different times; but you can also overlay onto existing illustrations to make them progressively more complex, control the speed at which text materials are printed on the screen, and pause for emphasis as materials are being printed on the screen. Because of the overlap, learners quickly perceive the interrelationships between the information provided on individual frames. By erasing only part of the screen, you can maintain information that remains constant, such as directions and student option information, and only change the instructional information.

On criterion frames, it is possible to erase only that portion of a student's response which is incorrect, focusing attention on the mistake. Figure 7.5 shows two frames. In the first frame the student made a mistake doing a computer-generated long division problem. In the second frame the computer alerted the student to the mistake and erased the incorrect portion so that they could try again.

When using the erase and overwrite capabilities, be careful not to unintentionally overwrite portions of a display you wished to preserve and to erase only the portion of the screen you intended to erase.

7.3 CONTROLLING THE RATE OF DISPLAY

One of your most important concerns should be the rate and method you are going to use to control the presentation of succeeding displays. While it is possible to have the rate of presentation automatically controlled by the computer, it is not advisable in most cases. Experience shows that, no matter for what rate you set the computer's automatic timer, it will be either too fast or too slow for most learners. For most circumstances, find ways to let the learner control the rate of presentation.

The most common way to control screen development is to force the learner to press a specific key before the next frame is displayed. The most popular are the SPACE BAR key and the Return/Enter key. The Return/Enter key is normally used to indicate the end of a learner's typed response. Therefore, I think the SPACE BAR is a better key to use when no additional response is required and the function is simply to control the turning of pages or frames.

No matter which key you choose, tell the learner what action to take in order to proceed forward in the program. Some authors feel it is sufficient to tell the learner at the beginning of the program what key to press, and then to use a flashing symbol of some type to tell the learner that the computer is ready to proceed when they are. A clearly stated "continue" message should be presented on every non-response screen. Its location and wording should be consistent throughout the program.

A simple message like "Press the SPACE BAR to continue . . . " placed on the bottom line of each screen, where no response is required, is enough to remind the learner what the computer is waiting for (see Figure 7.6). The use of all upper-case letters for the words "SPACE BAR" provides the learner with an immediate short prompt as to the proper key to press. The placement of this

Study the proper way
to set a table

Press the SPACE BAR to continue

Figure 7.6   Frame display under "SPACE BAR" control

message at the bottom of the screen is important for two reasons. In most Western societies people read from the upper left corner of the page, working their way down to the lower right corner. Placing the message at the bottom of the screen makes it the last thing the learner sees after all of the other information has been viewed. Second, this location is relatively inconspicuous. Learners who no longer need the prompt can ignore the message altogether, thus speeding up the presentation rate.

Where learners are required to generate an entered response, the SPACE BAR routine should not be used. Under no circumstance should a learner ever be required to press both the Return/Enter key and a SPACE BAR key in order to proceed with the program.

Automatic or computer-timed frame development may be used for nonessential frames such as the title frame. A good rule-of-thumb is to time how long it takes to read the frame out loud twice, and then to set the automatic timing device to that rate for that frame. Provide the learner with some type of manual override. Learners who go back through a program for review want to pass through frames quickly to get to the relevant frames. Otherwise they are forced to needlessly spend time waiting.

An automatically timed presentation rate may be advantageous when response feedback is very short. If all you are going to do is inform the learner that he/she got the response "Correct," then allow just enough time for the feedback to be read (about three seconds) and move on automatically. An automatic rate may also be used when additional portions of a display are going to be added without erasing what is already on the screen. This is called "progressive disclosure" and is very effective when complex materials are being presented. Figure 7.7 shows two frame displays. In the first, the clock face and text were placed on the screen for approximately four seconds (the time necessary to read the text through twice). The hour and minute hands were then added, the numbers on the clock face removed, and the student asked a question. By automatically disclosing information in this way, the numbers became a limited prompt for the learner's response, and the learner's attention was first drawn to the new piece of information before attention was shifted to the question.

In addition to controlling the forward rate of displays, CBI authors should consider providing learners an option for backing up one or more displays. A key or set of keys could be assigned for this purpose. For example, if the computer system you are designing for has arrow keys, these keys might be assigned to allow the learner to scan backward or forward through the displays until the desired display is located. If such option keys are available, the student should be informed of these options. Where possible, a short option reminder should be displayed on an inconspicuous part of the screen or on a permanent help frame. The bottom row of Figure 7.8 shows the option keys that are active while this frame is on the screen.

The question mark key (?) is often used to designate the need

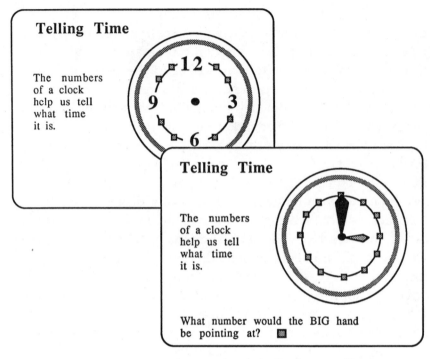

Figure 7.7   Automatic progressive disclosure displays

for help. Upon pressing this key, the learner could see an index showing the major subunits within the current lesson. From that index the learner could move forward or back to one of those subunits by entering the unit number and pressing ENTER. Figure 7.8 illustrates what this type of index might look like. Notice that the current position of the learner is marked with an arrow head as a referent point, and that other options are available from this menu. The procedures to follow when designing index/menus were discussed in Chapter 5.

7.4 USING FUNCTIONAL AREAS AND WINDOWS

The design of video displays should not be a process of random generation. Each piece of information that appears on the screen

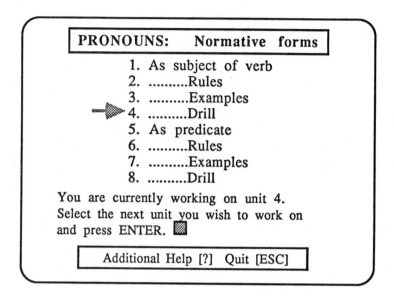

Figure 7.8 Index frame with option keys

should serve a particular function. Furthermore, the function served by each piece of information should be readily apparent to the learner. One way to help is to consistently use functional areas. A functional area is a portion of the video display screen where information relevant to that function appears each time it is required. The number and format of functional areas will vary from program to program, but their application within a program should be consistent.

Figure 7.9 shows a dialogue frame containing five functional areas. The area at the top of the screen contains the title and subtitle for the unit the learner is currently working on. Its main function is to keep the learner oriented within the program. The second functional area contains the instructional rule. In concept development, this is the information a learner needs to know in order to determine if a given example is or is not part of the concept (see Chapter 6). The third functional area provides the · learner with examples and non-examples of the rule or concept being taught. The fourth functional area's main function is to carry out a question, response, and feedback dialogue with the learner.

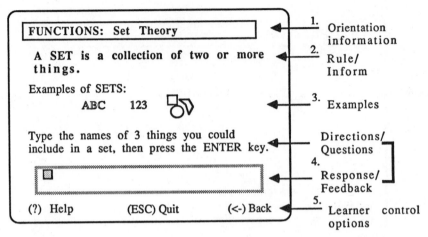

Figure 7.9 Using functional areas in display design

A fifth functional area appears at the bottom of the screen. It shows the "help" and other options currently available to the learner. All five areas shown in this frame were not used in every frame in the program; but, when used, they were generally located in the same position on the screen.

As discussed in the previous two chapters, frames serve different functions. So it is logical that the functional areas associated within a frame will differ according to the main function of the frame. There should be no hard and fast rule as to what a functional area should or should not present on a given frame. As a CBI author, you are in the best position for determining what information a learner will need and for coming up with some new functional areas. To help you get started, here is a list of some of the functional areas others have found useful.

Orientation information

As discussed earlier, the main purpose of this functional area is to keep the learner informed as to where he or she is in the program. In addition to providing a learner with a module title and subtitle, this functional area may be used to inform the learner of the current time of day, time spent on the lesson and on the current module, number of module segments completed and remaining to complete, and the current instructional mode, i.e., learning or review. At a minimum, orientation information should be provided on the first display of each section of a module.

When used on a frame, this functional area should be placed where it will not interfere with the overall subject matter presentation. In Figure 7.9, it was placed on the top line of the frame where it could be easily seen if needed but where it could be ignored once the learner goes into the main functions of the frame.

Directions

The directions function tells the learner what he or she is supposed to do in order to respond or proceed in the module. It may include a message as simple as "Press the SPACE BAR to continue..." or as detailed as an explanation of the type of response the computer is waiting for and the form in which the response should be typed. Some type of direction information should be present on every frame that is not automatically controlled by the computer. The fact that a set of general directions may be provided at the beginning of a program, or as part of the program documentation, does not eliminate the need for individual frame directions.

This functional information should also be placed in an area of the screen where it will not interfere with the teaching function, but it should be located so that when learners need the information they don't have to search for it. The best place is usually near the bottom of the screen, or just above the functional area where a learner's response is to be typed. Figure 7.9 shows the direction area just above the box where the learner will respond. Figure 7.10 has the direction area located on the last line of the frame, since no generated response is required.

Learner control options

A special type of direction is used to inform or remind the learner of the availability of program control options which are not di-

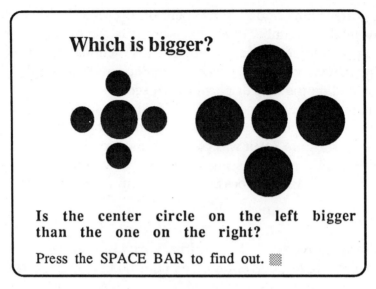

Figure 7.10   Bottom functional direction area

rectly related to the current frame but which may be accessed from the frame. These options may include the option to "Quit," to "BACKUP," to get "Help," or even to "Leave a Message" for the instructor. Where special keys are used to perform response editing or other learner response functions, the control option area could be used to remind the learner of the availability of these keys and the functions they serve.

Since control options are not directly a part of the main purpose of most frames, their functional area should be where it will not interfere with the continuity of the frame. The top or bottom line of the display appears to be the best location. However, when control options are an important part of the main function of the frame (e.g., if the frame is functioning as a word processor), and knowledge of the available options is critical to the learner's ability to correctly utilize the frame, then the options area should be conspicuous. Figure 7.11 shows two control option areas. The one at the top of the frame might be called a "passive" option area, because the information is supplemental to the main function of the frame and might not be used. The option area at the bottom

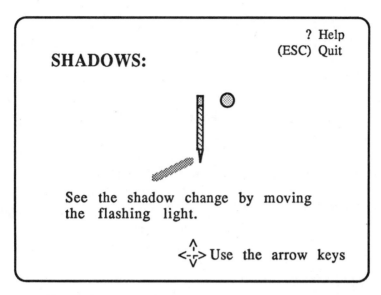

Figure 7.11   Active and passive option areas

is "active," showing the learner the option key to press to move the "flashing light" around the screen. Because of its importance to the main function of the frame, this portion of the option area should be placed in a conspicuous spot.

Rule/inform

The rule/inform area of a frame contains the background information and instructional rule which the learner is supposed to be learning from this and other related frames. In most instructional frames this functional area will take up most of the available frame space. Care should be exercised not to allow too much information to be placed on a single frame in this functional area. If the rule or background information is lengthy, it should be broken down into smaller, self-contained pieces and presented in a series of frames under learner control.

The rule/inform functional area need not contain "the facts and nothing but the facts." It should be motivational as well. It may include illustrated materials along with, or instead of, text information. Illustrated rules are sometimes more appropriate and effective than written rules, especially for younger and preschool-age children. Figure 7.11 shows a frame where the rule/inform functional area is limited to an illustration. The student is required to learn the rule by experimentation and evaluation of the information provided by the animated illustration without verbal prompt.

On criterion frames, the rule/inform area will usually contain the question or problem being tested. During early learning, it may be advisable to include both the general rule and a specific problem related to the rule so that children can begin to learn how to establish a relationship between the two.

Example/non-example

Most instruction requires the presentation of examples. A separate functional area may be set aside on the screen for this purpose. One reason for separating it from the rule/inform area is so that it can be erased and added to without affecting other areas of the screen. Using this technique, multiple examples and non-examples can be presented in succession without losing the continuity of the central concept rule. This area should be as close as possible to the rule/inform area, but without losing its individual identity. Items placed in this area should be clearly marked as "Examples" or "Non-Examples."

Response

The response functional area can serve two major purposes for the designer and the learner. First, it provides a location on the screen where the learner's response can be recorded. While it is possible to record a learner's response without showing it on the screen, learners need the visual feedback. They need to see it typed out to tell them not only that their response is being recorded but also that the response they thought they typed is the one the computer recorded. Even the best of typists sometimes hits the wrong key. The response function allows the learner to

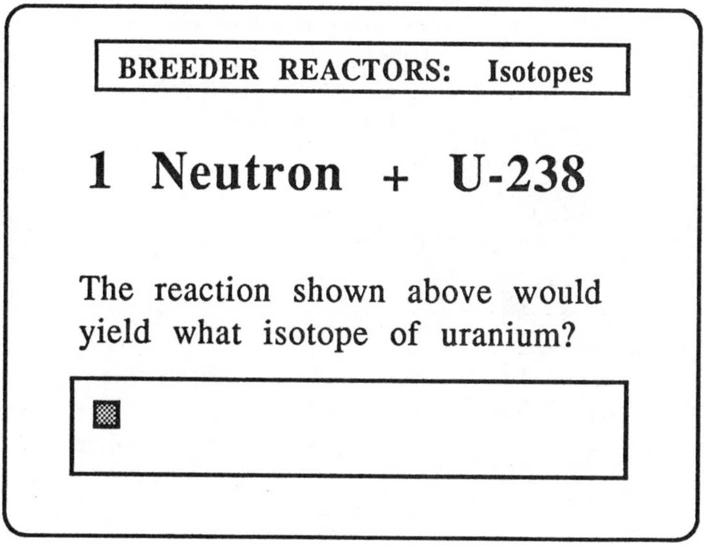

```
┌─────────────────────────────────────────┐
│   ┌───────────────────────────────────┐   │
│   │  BREEDER  REACTORS:   Isotopes    │   │
│   └───────────────────────────────────┘   │
│                                            │
│   1  Neutron  +  U-238                     │
│                                            │
│                                            │
│   The reaction shown above would           │
│   yield what isotope of uranium?           │
│                                            │
│   ┌───────────────────────────────────┐   │
│   │ ▨                                 │   │
│   │                                   │   │
│   └───────────────────────────────────┘   │
│                                            │
└─────────────────────────────────────────┘
```

Figure 7.12   Using a response window

see the response before it is finally sent and recorded in the computer's memory. For the functional area to serve this purpose, let the learner end the response by pressing the "Return/Enter" key.

Second, the response area can also be used to inform learners of the approximate size and/or type of response required. Figure 7.12 shows a frame where the response area is placed inside a box. The cursor inside the box marks the starting point, and the box itself shows the student the maximum size the response can be. The inside of the box is a window, which can be erased by the computer at will. This same frame can provide numerous practice opportunities without a box having to be formed for each trial.

Learners should not have to search for the response area. One important element of the response area is the cursor. All computer systems have some form of marker that indicates the location on the screen where the next piece of information will be typed. On most computers, the marker is a small white or patterned square or underline dash. The cursor usually flashes to catch the eye of

RAN JUMPED HE IS HOUSE
THE A OVER TO DOG BOY

From the list of words at the top of the
screen write a sentence that makes sense.
Put a period at the end of your sentence.

THE BOY RAN OVER THE DOG.

Figure 7.13   Interactive graphic feedback

the learner. When the computer is ready to receive a learner's
response, it is important that the cursor be located in the response
area.

Feedback/error message

One of the most important functional areas in any CBI program
is the area where learner feedback is provided. The feedback and
error message area provides a location on the screen where students can consistently look to find out if their response was correct
or incorrect, or where the computer can inform the learner of
problems it is having handling the learner's response, e.g. "Disk
too full to store response." The feedback/error area should only
be used for short messages. If longer messages are required, then
the rule/inform area should be used. Figure 7.13 shows an ex-

ample of this application. When a correct sentence was formed, the house and an animated dog and boy were used to reinforce the learning by acting out the sentence.

The feedback/error message area should be located on the screen adjacent to the response area, so learners see that the feedback is directly related to their response.

Generally, it is not possible nor advisable to use all of the functional areas described in this section on a single display. Nor is it important that, when they are used, they always be of exactly the same size, shape, and content. Their purpose is to let the learner spend time thinking about the content of a lesson rather than searching for relevant information.

Consistency in area placement also makes it possible for CBI designers and programmers to reuse display information. Earlier I said that the computer video screen is dynamic. If the designer desires, "windows," small independent subscreens, can be established as functional areas within the larger display. Each subscreen can be erased and written on without affecting the rest of the larger screen. This is an effective design technique. The use of a response area window makes it possible to erase an incorrect response without erasing the original question. In using this technique, leave enough room inside the window to allow the learner's complete response to be typed and the Return key to be pressed without scrolling any part of the response off the screen. Figure 7.14 shows a frame where five functional areas were used and three independent windows were programmed. Using this programming technique allowed the author of this frame to present new questions and/or new examples, and/or to give the learner a chance to respond again without having to erase any of the other functional areas on the screen.

While consistently using specific portions of a display for specific functions is important to good screen design, one note of caution should be made before we go on. Observation of numerous learners has made clear what happens when little detectable change in screen design occurs over even a short period

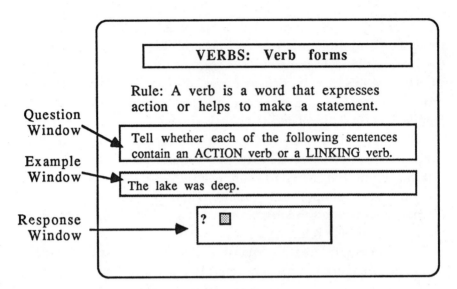

Figure 7.14   Using functional areas and windows to improve display efficiency

of time. Learners sometimes fail to realize that a new display has been placed on the screen, and they proceed right past it. It's like driving down a familiar street and not seeing a new house, because you're so used to seeing the street as it was. Getting past this problem is where your artistic ability comes in. Displays must be dynamic and exciting enough to continue to attract the attention of learners. Yet they must be consistently organized so that information can be conveyed in the most efficient and effective manner.

7.5 SUMMARY

Screen design is more an art than a science. To design effective screens, you should know something about communication and learning theory, human engineering, instructional message design, and art. Good screen design helps you attract a learner's attention and convey an intended message.

Computer generated video displays are generally far less sophisticated than normal television displays, but they can be far more sophisticated than a standard printed text display. Computer video displays are limited in resolution by the number of rows and columns of pixels they are able to produce. They are also limited in their ability to reproduce a complete range of colors. Computer screens are highly dynamic. Portions of the screen can be changed without affecting information on the remainder of the screen.

In terms of text characters, computer screens can normally generate either 40 or 80 character columns across and 24 character rows down. As much as 50 percent of the total screen space should remain blank at any given time. Break large quantities of text up with illustrations or into smaller, more manageable pieces.

The presentation of individual screens should generally be placed under learner control. The most common device is the SPACE BAR, or Return/Enter key, which is pressed before the next frame is shown. The learner should always be informed and reminded what action to take in order to proceed from frame to frame. Where possible, learners should be provided with the option to review previous displays.

Using functional areas is one of the best ways to organize displays. Functional areas which are often used in CBI design are: orientation areas, direction areas, rule/information areas, example areas, response areas, dialogue areas, feedback areas, and an options area.

- The orientation area is used to inform the learner where he or she is in the program.
- Direction areas tell learners what they are supposed to do to respond or proceed in the program.
- An options area reminds the learner of the availability of program control options.
- Rule/information areas provide the learner with information and/or stimulus materials.

- Example/non-example functional areas present positive and negative examples of the information or skill to be learned.
- Response areas provide a location where the learner's response can be recorded and where short feedback messages can be provided by the computer.
- Feedback/error message areas keep the learner informed of results and/or problems the computer may have in handling responses.

Placing functional areas inside an independently controlled screen window in consistent ways permits the reuse or review of individual screen segments and makes programming more efficient.

7.6 ISSUES AND ACTIVITIES

1. Using the five most popular brands of computers in your area, make a list comparing the screen and display capabilities of each brand.
2. Use a layout sheet similar to those shown at the end of Chapter 8 to design a series of displays for a program you are planning to write.
3. Take a single page from an average instructional textbook and determine how many computer screens it would take to display all the material on the single page.
4. Observe a few learners as they go through a CBI program. Using a stop watch, time how long each individual remains on a few of the frames. Is there a great deal of consistency between individual users? What are the implications?
5. Analyze a CBI program to determine what functional areas were used. Can you think of ways that the program could have been made more efficient by increasing the number of functional areas or by using independently controlled windows?

7.7 REFERENCES

Fleming, M., & Levie, H. *Instructional Message Design: Principles from the Behavioral Sciences.* Englewood Cliffs, NJ: Educational Technology Publications, 1978.

Hanks, K., Belliston, L., & Edwards, D. *Design Yourself!* Los Altos, CA: William Kaufmann, 1978.

Heines, J. M. *Screen Design: Strategies for Computer-Assisted Instruction.* Bedford, MA: Digital Equipment Corp., 1984.

Kamins, S., & Waite, M. *Apple Backpack: Humanized Programming in BASIC.* Peterborough, NH: BYTE/McGraw-Hill, 1982.

Markle, S. M. *Good Frames and Bad: A Grammar of Frame Writing.* New York: John Wiley & Sons, 1969.

Merrill, M. D., & Tennyson, R. D. *Teaching Concepts: An Instructional Design Guide.* Englewood Cliffs, NJ: Educational Technology Publications, 1977.

Meyers, J., & Tognazzini, B. *Design Guidelines.* Cupertino, CA: Apple Computer, 1982.

Minnesota Educational Computing Consortium. *Designing Instructional Computing Materials.* St. Paul, MN: Author, 1982.

Taylor, R. P. *The Computer in the School: Tutor, Tool, Tutee.* New York: Teachers College Press, 1980.

Turnbull, A. T., & Baird, R. N. *The Graphics of Communication.* New York: Holt, Rinehart & Winston, 1975.

8

Using Text and Graphics

8.0 INTRODUCTION

A CBI program is really just a packaged form of communication. We all communicate every day by the way we dress, by the way we stand or walk, and by the way we smile. Much of our communication is informal and automatic. Many times we are totally unaware of the messages that others are getting from us. Silence may be one of the "loudest" forms of communication we can send, if conditions are right. The words we speak are just one element of the total process involved in interpersonal communication. Unfortunately, when we must transform interpersonal communication into a format the computer can generate, we bypass the facial expressions, gestures, and tonal inflections that play such an important role in our face-to-face communications. In designing CBI programs, we are, in general, limited to just a few elements, such as the written word (text) and simple illustrations (graphics).

The fact that only a limited number of elements are available to us does not mean that our communication has to be boring or ineffective. Almost everyone who reads has had the experience of staying up late at night to finish a book that contains nothing more than letters printed on plain white paper. Many people spend thousands of dollars purchasing pictures that consist of colored oil on pieces of rough canvas. Obviously it's not the paper or paint that limits the writer's or artist's ability to communicate, it's how creative they are in using and combining those elements that makes the difference.

As a CBI designer, you need to learn what tools and elements make up a CBI program; and then you must learn to apply your creative talents to manipulate those elements in the most effective manner possible. In this chapter we are going to focus on two of the elements that make up your computer displays. The text portion includes your written words, along with the other signs and symbols that have come to be associated with our written language. The graphic portions of a display include not only illustrations but the general layout of the entire display, including the careful design and placement of text.

While text and graphics are the tools and elements you use, the effectiveness of your program will not be judged on them but on how creatively and how well you use them to communicate.

8.1 USING TEXT IN SCREEN DISPLAYS

Text, the written word, makes up 80 to 90 percent of most CBI program frame displays. Even so, most CBI designers spend little time making design decisions that involve the text portion of the screen. This is because they assume that they have very little choice as to what the text is to look like or where and how it is to be placed on the screen. Neither of these assumptions is true.

The first consideration the designer has control over is the amount of text that is to be presented to the learner in a single frame. A computer cannot replace a book. Whenever large quantities of text are required as part of a learning experience, give the learner a printed copy of that material. Experience and research has shown that learners cannot hold large quantities of text in their heads. No matter how important all that information is, let the computer handle only that portion of it that requires inter- action. Let a printed supplement handle the rest.

The quantity of text provided the learner and the form of that text involves both the larger CBI program and the individual frames. Within a CBI frame there are guidelines which help con- vey the desired information by improving the readability and legibility of the text. There are also guidelines which, if utilized, help attract and hold the learner's attention on the text portion of the page.

The use of "space," the empty portions of a display, may be the most powerful tool a text screen designer has. In Figure 7.3 in the previous chapter you saw a text frame in which all available space was filled with text. Such displays have been found to cause reading fatigue and to be extremely tiring to the eyes. Research has shown that a learner's eyes seem to seek a place to rest when looking at large quantities of video text material. Sometimes that resting place is a margin, sometimes it's an illustration, and some- times it's an empty area in the middle of the screen. When the eye and mind can't find that resting point within a frame, the eye goes elsewhere, and the mind wanders away from the computer lesson. Some research suggests that, for this and other reasons, as much as 50 percent of a frame should be blank space. This includes margins, space between lines of text, space between let- ters and words, and space within illustrations.

Space is also used to organize information. If all the letters of a sentence were equally spaced, it would be difficult to read them, e.g., thisisjustagroupofletters. When we add more space between some of the letters we begin to form words, e.g., this is more than just a group of letters. The frame shown in Figure 8.1 is made up of similar shaped boxes. Even though the basic content is similar in appearance, it is easy to see that some of the boxes are more closely related than others, largely because of the space between them.

Space can be used to organize and group ideas and functions in a text frame. Figure 8.2 shows a frame in which single, double, and triple spacing has been used to group ideas into separate units and to separate the "information" function of the frame

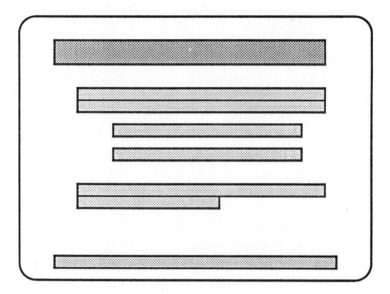

Figure 8.1   Use of space in frame design

Verbs: Present   infinitives

Use the present infinitive (to go, to see, etc.)
to express action following another action.

> Wrong   He intended to have gone with
> us.
> Right   He intended to go with us.

Type the following sentence correctly and
press the ENTER key:
> **He hoped to have written to**
> **each   child.**

Figure 8.2   Space defines function

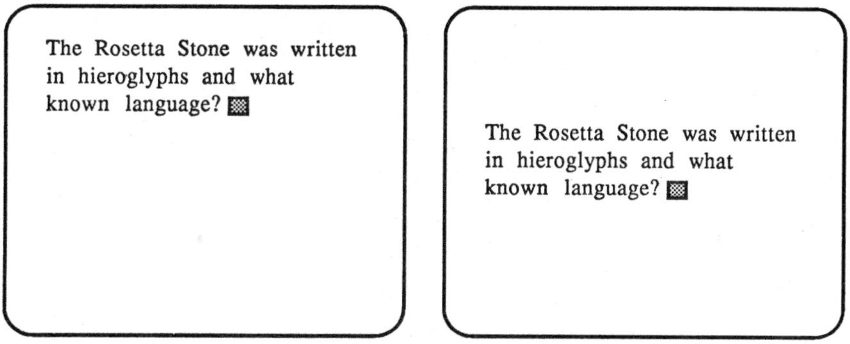

The Rosetta Stone was written in hieroglyphs and what known language? ▓

The Rosetta Stone was written in hieroglyphs and what known language? ▓

Figure 8.3   Centering text on the screen

from the "question/response" function. The "title" function and "option" function are also set apart from the main functions of the frame by the use of space, position on the screen, and a border.

Like illustrated displays, text displays should be artistically pleasing. One of the most common faults with text screens is the crowding of materials against the top of the screen. When designing text screens, center the text and stay away from the margins. Figure 8.3 shows two screens, one where the programmer took the easy way out and allowed the computer to print text from the upper left-hand corner—the "home" position—on down the page. Because the amount of material is small, the screen appears under-used, that is, there is too much blank space in one area. The second frame has corrected the problem. It is much more interesting and pleasing to the eye.

When a text screen becomes too full, or when text material reaches the bottom row of the screen, the screen appears to "scroll." Scrolling is the process used by the computer to push lines of text up on the screen in order to make room for new lines of text at the bottom. CBI designers should never permit a screen to get so full that scrolling occurs.

One time scrolling occurs is when a learner's response is being entered. Even though a response may be very short, if poorly placed on the screen it can cause the entire screen to scroll or a single line to be divided in an unpredictable way. The culprit in these situations is usually the Return/Enter key.

The Return key is an important part of the learner's response since, on most computer systems, it adds what is called a "line feed" to the response. The line feed has the effect of adding one blank line to the response by moving the cursor (the small flashing box) down one line below the last line typed. If the last line typed is either the bottom line of the screen or the bottom line of a window discussed earlier, the effect of the line feed is to cause the screen or window to scroll. Designers must allow one extra line at the bottom of the screen or window to account for this factor.

The use of a learner's response along with other preprogrammed text can cause other problems for the text designer. Most programming languages do not provide ongoing text formatting capabilities. That is, once the computer has been told how long a line should be, if the number of characters in that line exceeds the number of characters the computer can print on a single line, the computer moves the excess letters down to the next line. When moving those letters it does not normally break them at a word break and it does not normally combine the leftover letters with the line that follows. It simply leaves them dangling on a line all by themselves. Figure 8.4 shows a frame where a learner's response, their name, was inserted in the middle of a preprogrammed text. On this 40 column screen the designer allowed 8 extra spaces for the learner's first name. Unfortunately this learner's name "Anne Marie," which was typed in at the beginning of the program, required 10 spaces. As a result, the learner's name got split into two parts and the screen was left with a dangling sentence fragment.

Until recently, the length of a text line on a computer video display was not something most designers had to worry about. The only choice they had on most instructional computers was a 40 or 80 character-wide display. With new programming techniques and improved hardware capabilities, this is no longer the case. Even programs written for older computers can be set up for different line lengths. Until more research is done on the effect

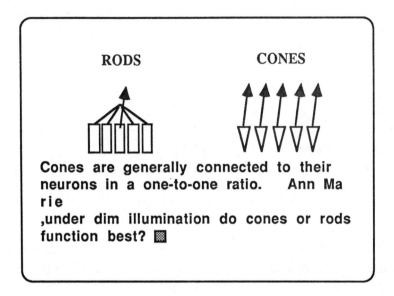

Figure 8.4   Mixing variable and pre-programmed text

of line length on the readability of video displays, some useful guidelines from the traditional print field can be applied here.

The major concern is to achieve a line short enough to permit the learner to scan it with a minimal amount of head movement and at the same time long enough to allow for the fewest number of broken or hyphenated words or thought units. Both head movement and broken words slow down reading speed and cause a loss of sentence continuity. The standard rule of thumb in the print field is to provide approximately 50 to 70 characters per line, with an average of 65.

The width of space between lines also affects the readability of the text. Some authors believe that double spacing all text material improves readability. This author feels it breaks up the unity of sentences and ideas. Instead of using double spacing throughout a text frame, I suggest you use it selectively to emphasize major ideas or breaks in thought. Figure 8.5 shows two frames, one where all the text is double spaced and one where spacing is used for emphasis and unity of ideas. Either technique may be effective in a given situation.

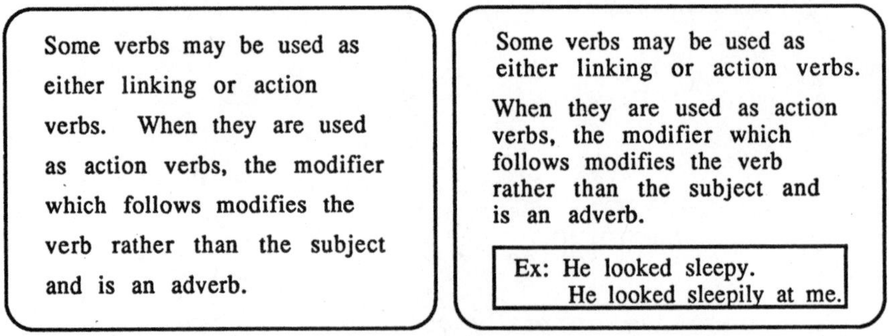

Some verbs may be used as either linking or action verbs. When they are used as action verbs, the modifier which follows modifies the verb rather than the subject and is an adverb.

Some verbs may be used as either linking or action verbs.

When they are used as action verbs, the modifier which follows modifies the verb rather than the subject and is an adverb.

Ex: He looked sleepy.
He looked sleepily at me.

Figure 8.5   Line spacing of text material

The length and spacing of text lines is affected by the size and boldness of the type being used. Most computer systems presently on the market provide options for printing different type styles and sizes. When this option is available, designers should consider some of the following in making text style and size decisions:

Consider larger type sizes when designing programs for younger children.   Care should be taken, however, not to use overly large type. Large, poorly spaced type can cause younger readers to see only individual letters, not words. The frame shown in Figure 8.6 was filled with only one word. But most younger readers were unable to form the word, even though they learned to read it in another context. If a single word requires more than a single eye fixation, it is highly likely that the learner will misread the word.

Use both upper- and lowercase letters.   All uppercase letters works fine for titles, but for many reasons it slows down reading and often causes young readers not to recognize words they are otherwise familiar with.

Use boldface and color type for emphasis but not for the main body of the text.   Boldface type tends to cause the space between letters to fill in. On poor-quality monitors and televisions, this may make some of the text illegible. Bold type also causes what is sometimes

Figure 8.6   Improper use of oversized type

called "sparkle." The letters appear to flash very rapidly. This is hard to look at for any length of time and the learner usually turns the display off.

If it's available, use a serif lettering style rather than a block or sans serif style.   Serif letters have "feet" (serifs) which extend from the bottom and sometimes the top of the letters. Block or sans serif letters are generally squared or rounded off at the bottom. Figure 8.7 shows an example of these two lettering styles. The added lines of the serif style increase the readability of text displays and make the letters more interesting to the eye.

Figure 8.7   Major lettering styles

Use special text effects for emphasis only. Most computers are capable of generating a wide variety of special text effects, ranging from flashing letters to italics. If used sparingly, these techniques can be effective. They call attention to an important point, wake a student up, or set off a special functional area. Some of these special effects, their advantages and disadvantages, are listed below:

- **Inverse video**—Helpful in creating a distinction between two kinds of information that appear on a screen. Can be hard to read on poor quality TVs.
- **Italic and bold letters**—Helpful in emphasizing single words and titles.
- **Flashing or blinking characters**—Wake up the learner's senses. Useful for short messages to inform the learner that the computer is busy but is still working. Very hard to look at and read for any length of time.
- **Boxing around text**—Useful in setting off functional areas such as student response area. May be used to dress up an otherwise dull-appearing text page.
- **Colored letters and symbols**—Adds excitement to titles. Focuses attention on an area of text or portion of an illustration. Works best on larger sizes of text. Should normally not be used for the main body of text.
- **Underlining**—Helpful in emphasizing groups of words and titles. Not available on most computers.
- **Moving "billboard" text**—Text moves horizontally across the screen, usually repeating the same message with each pass. Useful for putting messages which are longer than a single screen width on a single line. Helpful when a large number of option keys are available and option messages must continually be presented on the screen without using up a lot of screen display space.

8.2 USING GRAPHIC METAPHORS

As discussed in Chapter 4, humans work best in a familiar environment, or one that contains elements they can easily associate

Figure 8.8   International symbols

with previous experiences and environments. One of the most effective tools used for making the unfamiliar familiar is the metaphor. A metaphor is a figurative expression that implies a comparison by associating two objects or ideas that are usually not associated but that can be made to appear so in a reader's or viewer's imagination. Phrases like "busy as a bee" or "the gas-guzzling dinosaurs of the road" make abstract concepts live.

Like verbal metaphors, visual metaphors also help us understand something unfamiliar. International symbols such as those shown in Figure 8.8 tell us where we can find a phone, exchange money, or get a drink. Such visual metaphors are extremely useful in helping computer users find their way around the often-confusing environment of CBI.

The visual metaphor used in organizing computer displays was first developed by XEROX on its Star office automation system. In recent years the concept has been popularized by Apple's Macintosh and Commodor's Amiga systems. The use of the visual metaphor by such systems is not limited to a single or even a few specific symbols. The visual metaphor becomes the working environment within which all the program functions operate. The now famous Macintosh "desktop," with its icons and waste basket, provides a working area that is familiar to almost anyone who works in an office environment. We all know that the computer doesn't really have a desktop or a waste basket, but we are willing to go along with such a familiar operating environment.

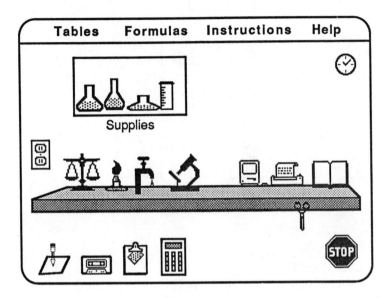

Figure 8.9   Learning lab metaphor

This same desktop metaphor is also an effective metaphor for education, but it is not the only user environment in which learning occurs. Figure 8.9 illustrates a learning lab metaphor, where icons represent most of the major tools a learner in this environment might want access to. To access these resources, all the learner has to do is point the mouse at the familiar icon and click. As the learner selects an icon, the mental image created by the basic lab metaphor is carried forward, in a consistent manner, to more specific metaphors that relate to that selection.

Figure 8.10 illustrates a learning metaphor used in teaching a foreign language. The metaphor, in this instance, is a village in which the learner must learn to cope and utilize the language skills developed elsewhere in the program. As the learner selects a building to enter, the computer presents the learner with other metaphors and problems which relate to language development in a specific context. The CBI program where this metaphor was used was integrated with an interactive videodisc system. The materials contained on the videodisc make the metaphor seem even more realistic to the user. After selecting an icon from the

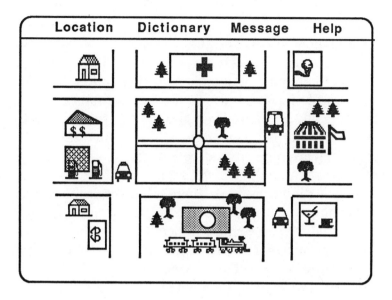

Figure 8.10 Language instruction metaphor

metaphor, the learner encounters actual pictures of clerks and taxi drivers asking questions and providing realistic interactions.

While technology such as the videodisc does add realism to the metaphor, such realism is not essential. The metaphor may present an environment quite different from reality without losing its effectiveness. When you use visual metaphors in CBI programs, the purpose is not to help the learner understand reality but to make the unfamiliar world of the computer fit into the real world as currently understood by the learner.

8.3 USING PICTURES AND GRAPHICS

Inexpensive computers can now generate illustrated and graphic images. This advancement is fairly recent and very important to the application of computers in the instructional environment. Graphics and other forms of illustration can serve many purposes for the CBI designer. One of the most significant is to attract and hold a learner's attention. An interesting illustration not only attracts attention to itself but also to the text portion of the page. Learners generally are more likely to read text that is associated with an illustration than they are to read unrelated text.

Illustrations are remembered better than text. This fact does not mean that we should, or could, replace all of the text portions of our frames with illustrations. There is a great deal of evidence to suggest, however, that the better a learner can associate an idea or concept with some type of concrete image, the more likely the learner will remember that idea or concept. Use illustrations for visual reinforcement of abstract concepts. Don't illustrate every frame, and don't include illustrations that don't add to the central purpose of the frame. If a meaningful graphic or illustration can be designed to enhance the frame's central message, then it should be considered.

Diagrams, charts, and illustrations help learners synthesize and organize information. For example, the water cycle is a complex process with numerous subprocesses. A diagram can help a learner organize all of these subprocesses in order to understand both their temporal and their functional relationships to the overall process. Unlike text material, which must be read one word at a time, concepts presented visually can be processed simultaneously. Relationships then become more evident.

The old saying, "a picture is worth a thousand words," may not always be true. But illustrations do add to our understanding, and they help us to avoid the overuse of technical jargon. It should be pointed out, though, that there are times when a single word may be worth a thousand pictures. If a learner already understands what the word "tree" means, it would be a waste of valuable resources to illustrate the concept, especially when you consider all of the different types of trees that learners have already stored away in their mind. Use illustrations only in those instances where a common usage of language does not already exist.

Figure 8.11   Computer generated graphics
(From Lisa Art Department by Apple Computer Inc.)

Computers cannot generate all of the illustrative materials that we would sometimes like in a CBI lesson. Most computer systems are limited to illustrations made up of lines and symbols. They cannot reproduce lifelike representations we are used to seeing on film and television. It is possible to connect computer systems to video recorders and videodisc players and intermix computer generated displays with these more realistic displays. Such systems are still relatively expensive, but they are currently being used in many industrial and military instructional environments. For the purposes of this text, we will limit our discussion to the types of illustrations that the computer itself can generate.

Figure 8.11 shows a collection of illustration types which a computer can generate. Included in this collection are line illustrations, graphs, charts, symbols, and animations.

If you follow just a few simple guidelines when using graphic illustrations in your frames, you can increase the effectiveness of these illustrations.

- **Keep illustrations appropriate to your intended audience.** Cute cartoon illustrations don't have the same effect on adults as they do on children.
- **Simple line drawings are generally preferred to complex pictorial illustrations.** When complex illustrations are required, you should build them up on the screen one step at a time so that the learner can analyze all of the relevant parts. Highlight important areas of complex graphics.
- **Create graphics quickly, unless progressive disclosure is to be used for concept development.** Preload graphics. Don't make the learner wait while the computer goes to the disk drive to get the graphic file. When the graphic is to be drawn on the screen, use a "quick draw" programming technique.
- **Use standard symbols and symbolic representations as much as possible.** Visual literacy is a learned skill. Make sure your audience understands the symbols and representations you use in your illustrations.
- **When you use color for coding, always provide a backup pattern for those who may not have access to a color monitor or TV.** Color can be a very effective tool in designing computer displays, but sometimes things outside the control of the designer will negate the value of color, causing it at times to work against the overall quality of the program. Many instructional units do not have color televisions available for all of their computers, and a sizeable part of the population is color blind. You will need to provide shaded patterns, or different-shaped symbols, so that your program can be used on these computers or by these individuals. Check out your program on a black and white or monochromatic monitor to be sure that your use of color does not void the use of the program on other output systems. Color does add a great deal to the motivational quality of a program, especially for young children.
- **Animations should be short and appropriate.** Animations are highly effective for attracting a learner's attention to a portion of a screen, but they can be distracting if left on too long. Animations designed to illustrate the motion involved

in a particular process, e.g., the operation of an internal combustion engine, should be interruptable by the learner, and the speed of the animation should be learner controlled as much as possible. Animation can be very effective as a reward for a correct response if it is not overused.

- **Avoid providing too many images on a single frame.** Like text, too many illustrations on a single frame only confuses the learner. Where possible, a printed copy of complex illustrations should be provided for the learner's use after leaving the CBI program.

- **Place illustrations as close as possible to the related text material, but never on a display that precedes the related text.** When it is necessary to separate the text and a related illustration, place the illustration frame immediately after the text frame(s). If possible, provide a way for the learner to move back and forth between the text and illustration frames. When text and graphic are included on the same frame, program the computer to print the text portion of the frame on the screen before the graphic portion, unless the text and graphic are a single unit.

The inclusion of graphics in an instructional program need not be a difficult or burdensome project. In recent years, many companies have made available graphic and character set libraries which, when purchased and licensed, can be used freely within their instructional programs.

8.4 TOOLS FOR DESIGNING DISPLAYS

The design of effective video displays is not something that should be left to the programmer. If you are the programmer, don't wait until the programming stage of development. Carefully plan out your displays in advance. A technique of film and video producers called "storyboarding" is useful in this regard. It is a process of doing rough sketches for each frame to be presented. Figures 8.12

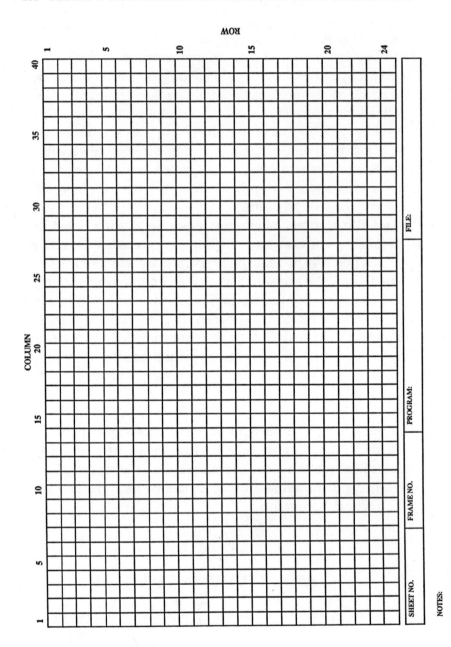

Figure 8.12   40 column display worksheet

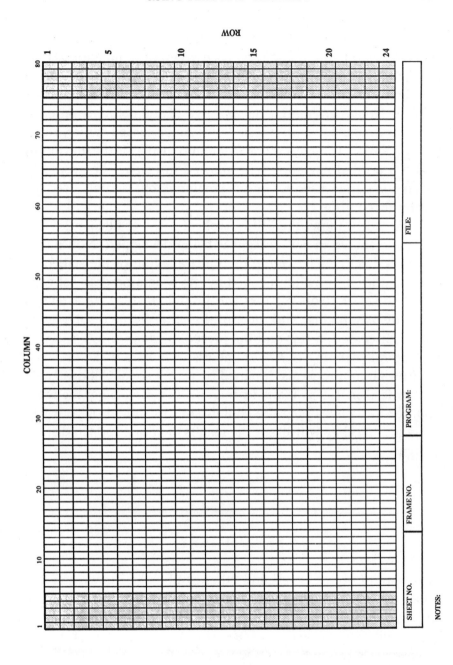

Figure 8.13   80 column display worksheet

and 8.13 show sample worksheets which this author uses for this purpose. Figure 8.12 is the form used when designing for a computer that uses a 40 column display. Figure 8.13 is used when working with a computer that can generate a 65 or larger column display. Notice in Figure 8.13 that five of the columns on each end of the sheet have been shaded in. As discussed earlier, readability standards suggest that a 70 column display is the maximum length a printed line should be allowed to reach. The grayed-in area is sometimes used for graphic material, but is rarely used for text by this author.

Figure 8.14 shows the CBI worksheet that was filled out when the frame shown in Figure 7.4 was being developed. Notice that the worksheet contains more than just a layout of the screen. It also includes information needed by the programmer to set windows, to select colors for text and graphic display, to establish frame display timing, and most of the other frame display techniques discussed in this and the preceding chapter.

Careful planning of CBI frame displays may make or break your program. Programs designed by professional CBI designers *look* professional. Few if any learners will ever see all of the work you put into developing the content and treatment of your CBI program, but they will all see the results of your efforts in display design.

8.5 SUMMARY

Text in the form of words and other symbols of the written language make up as much as 80 to 90 percent of the information displayed by CBI programs. The remaining 10 to 20 percent consists of illustrations and other forms of graphics. Since these are the elements through which we communicate, it is essential for CBI designers to understand some of the characteristics associated with these elements as they are displayed by a computer.

Computers should not be used to replace a printed book. Where large quantities of text are required, a printed document

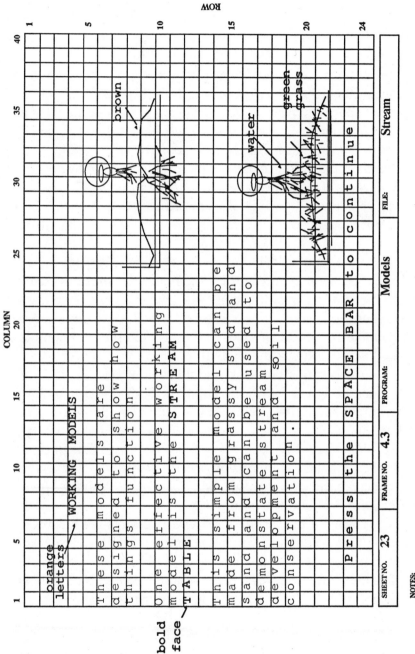

**Figure 8.14 Worksheet for CBI frame on "soil erosion model"
(see Figure 7.4)**

should be included with the courseware package. Only highly interactive portions of a lesson should be programmed on a computer.

Screen displays should never be entirely filled with text. As much as 50 percent of a display should be blank space, including borders, space between text lines, and space surrounding text and graphic elements. Space is one of the best ways of organizing functional areas and highlighting important information.

Text scrolling is one of the biggest problems faced by designers and learners. Unless designed for special purposes, text should never be allowed to scroll. Plan ahead so that a learner's input does not cause a screen to scroll or lines to be split in uncontrolled ways.

For maximum readability, text lines should be kept between 50 and 70 characters in length. If the line is too short, the learner loses the continuity of the sentence. Likewise, lines that are too long cause learners to lose track of where they are on the frame.

Double spacing is effective for young children, but it tends to slow down and break the thought pattern of adults.

The use of large type fonts should be limited to headlines and programs designed for young children. Both upper- and lower-case letters should be used. Boldface type should be used only for emphasis, not for the main body of the text. Serif letter styles, if available, should be used for text. Use other special effect letter styles sparingly for emphasis or variety. Readability and legibility decrease rapidly with the use of special text forms such as inverse letters and flashing or blinking letters.

Graphics are one of the most effective tools we have for attracting and holding a learner's attention. Graphics are also remembered better than text materials. They are an excellent way to summarize and cut down the amount of required text. Diagrams, charts, and illustrations help learners synthesize and organize information.

Illustrations should be appropriate for the intended audience. Simple line drawings are generally preferred to complex pictorial illustrations. Standard symbols and symbolic representations should be used as much as possible. Colored illustrations should be designed so that they can be effectively used on a black and white or "green screen" monitor without loss to the intended message. Text and illustrations should be related together into meaningful learning experiences.

CBI designers should develop "storyboard" worksheets, detailing each element of the program's major frames. The worksheet should include all the information that will be required during the programming process.

8.6 ISSUES AND ACTIVITIES

1. Design a series of instructional frames using the worksheets shown in Figures 8.12 and 8.13. Have them critiqued by someone knowledgeable in graphic layout. People trained in advertising layout are especially good at this.
2. Locate a CBI program that has good content ideas but poor. display design. Redesign several of the frames to make them more interesting and to improve the overall effectiveness of the message.
3. Take a page of text from a typical textbook and see how much you can reduce the number of words used without losing the major messages conveyed on the page.
4. Talk with someone who is knowledgeable on the computer you have or are planning to design for. Find out all you can about the variety of text and graphic options that can be provided that computer system. If necessary write or phone the computer company and ask their technical support staff for help and information in this area. You may be able to make use of computer features that you didn't know existed.
5. Compare various computer systems to determine which system offers the best text and graphic capabilities.

8.7 REFERENCES

Fleming, M., & Levie, H. *Instructional Message Design: Principles from the Behavioral Sciences.* Englewood Cliffs, NJ: Educational Technology Publications, 1978.

Hanks, K., Belliston, L., & Edwards, D. *Design Yourself!* Los Altos, CA: William Kaufmann, 1978.

Heines, J. M. *Screen Design: Strategies for Computer-Assisted Instruction.* Bedford, MA: Digital Equipment Corp., 1984.

Jonassen, D. *The Technology of Text: Principles for Structuring, Designing, and Displaying Text.* Englewood Cliffs, NJ: Educational Technology Publications, 1981.

Kamins, S., & Waite, M. *Apple Backpack: Humanized Programming in BASIC.* Peterborough, NH: BYTE/McGraw-Hill, 1982.

Meyers, J., & Tognazzini, B. *Design Guidelines.* Cupertino, CA: Apple Computer, 1982.

Minnesota Educational Computing Consortium. *Designing Instructional Computing Materials.* St. Paul, MN: Author, 1982.

Taylor, R. P. *The Computer in the School: Tutor, Tool, Tutee.* New York: Teachers College Press, 1980.

Turnbull, A. T., & Baird, R. N. *The Graphics of Communication.* New York: Holt, Rinehart & Winston, 1975.

9

Program
Documentation and
Support Materials

9.0 INTRODUCTION

The finished program disk is just one part of your total CBI course-ware package. Every package you design should include some form of printed program documentation. The documentation, usually in the form of a user manual, should at least tell the user:

- Where the program came from.
- What the program is intended to do.
- The minimum hardware requirements for successful program operation.
- How the program is loaded and executed on the computer.
- How to operate all of the major components that make up the program.

This sounds easy enough, but the absence of documentation, or the presence of nonuser-oriented documentation, is usually where most CBI programs fail. The most problems seem to occur when the documentation writer fails to understand the needs, interests, and abilities of the audience they are writing for.

The fact is that CBI documentation is rarely, if ever, written for just one audience. In education there are at least two audiences, teachers and learners. Teachers appreciate a lot of background information so that they know where and how to fit the CBI program into the total lesson. Learners, on the other hand, are mainly concerned with the actual operation of the program and what they personally can get out of it. And within these two groups are major differences in computer expertise and understanding. CBI documentation is best when it meets the needs of both audiences without providing too much or too little information to either.

Before we get into the actual content of the documentation, let's look a little more closely at your potential audiences. If you are writing a documentation manual to accompany a CBI program, you're probably not writing for programmers or experienced users who understand things like baud rate, "boot," or peripheral cards. This does not mean that the users of your program are not bright or knowledgeable in some other field, only that, in most cases, they are not technically expert in the use and terminology of computers.

Your audience selected your program because they needed to teach, learn, or practice something in the shortest way possible. No matter how good your program is, they are not there to linger. They came with a purpose, and they expect your program and its manual to help them accomplish it with as little effort as possible on their part. They certainly don't expect to have to become computer experts in order to use your program. Many are not technical thinkers. They don't concern themselves with abstract or theoretical matters. They are concerned with the solution of today's problems and the direct application of newly learned knowledge and skills.

Most of all, your audience is made up of individuals who expect to be treated with dignity and understanding. Documentation should be aimed at the individual, not the group. No matter how academically sophisticated they may be, they will appreciate easy, jargon-free reading. If they want to read themselves to sleep, let them do it with a good novel, not your documentation. Manuals should provide only information that is essential to the effective use of your program, so don't make it a textbook on computer literacy.

Not all documentation is, or should be, designed for a non-technical audience, however. There are individuals out there who may need a more technical explanation of your program so that they can maintain it, modify it to meet local needs, or interface it with other CBI or CMI programs or hardware. If you are going to allow such options, you may need to provide technical documentation in addition to the user manual discussed in the first part of this chapter. In the final section of this chapter we discuss some of the information to include in the more technical parts of your documentation. For now, let's discuss what should be included, and how you should design your nontechnical user manual.

9.1 ORGANIZING THE DOCUMENTATION

If you have been carrying out all of the steps described thus far, you probably have a pretty good technical grasp of every aspect of your program. If you are a programmer, you even have some technical understanding of what will be required to set up the necessary data files, input/output operations, and general program control. In a very real sense you are the expert on your program. The fact that you know so much about your program is exactly why it's going to be difficult for you to design and write a documentation manual to accompany it. Documentation manuals need to be written for users, not experts. Organizing the manual according to Input/Output options, CBI strategy, program management, etc., makes little sense to users, even though perfectly logical to you at this point. A basic rule I emphasize throughout this chapter is, Organize and write the program documentation around what the users will do or are expected to do with your program. Anticipate their needs and the questions they will ask. Organize the manual to answer questions like:

- What do I need to do to make it work?
- How do I get started?
- What are the rules of the game?
- What keys can I press?

If you really think you need to include all the technical information you collected in designing the program, then put it in an appendix or technical section at the back of the manual where the teacher, or learner, can access it if they feel a need for it. Keep the manual as simple as possible without leaving out any information that is going to make the operation of your program easier and more effective.

The first part of your manual should include some introductory pages, such as:

- A title page—so users can associate the manual with its accompanying computer software.
- A table of contents—so users can get where they want to go without having to become detectives.
- A preface—to help learners or others use the manual more effectively.
- An introduction—to provide users with an overview of both the manual and the accompanying computer software.

In most CBI documentation, the core of the manual must really be designed for two audiences. At least one section should be aimed directly at the learner and at what he/she needs to know in order to operate the program. It should be organized as a "stand alone" section, which the teacher can copy and give to learners prior to their use of the program. A separate section should meet the needs of the teacher, parent, or other individual who may be controlling the use of your product. The needs of each group differ. Providing just the right information for each group will be the topic of the next section of this chapter.

The central portion of the manual should be followed by a reference section. The reference section might include:

- A glossary—where new terms used in either the manual or the program are defined and explained.
- An index—providing the reader quick access to information on terms, commands, keys, and menu items referred to in the manual.
- A quick-reference card—which the teacher or learner can tear out and, if necessary, copy so that it can be placed next to the keyboard while the program is being utilized.

In CBI documentation, a fourth section might be provided to specifically help teachers and others who have to integrate and implement your program into the learning environment. Providing a section that includes additional instructional support materials and suggested activities can help guarantee that your program will be implemented in the way you hoped it would.

Depending on program modification and other options you provided for in your program, a fifth and final section might be the technical documentation you, the programmer, and other technical experts collected throughout the program's development. This can be of help in modifying or implementing your program on equipment or in ways specific to the user's needs.

9.2 INTRODUCTORY PAGES

Disclaimer page

If you look at the manuals that come with most computer software, you will see that the first few pages look very much alike. The first might be called the "disclaimer" page. If you have not written or produced a number of commercially sold programs, this page may appear to you as just a bunch of legal mumbo-jumbo. However, now that you are becoming a CBI developer, you should become more aware of what all those legal terms mean and include them in your own manuals. They may be your best protection against lawsuits and copyright infringements.

The disclaimer page usually includes a paragraph or two under the subtitle of "Limited Warranty." The warranty states the legal rights you are willing to grant the purchaser of your product and/or those rights the program purchaser has under state and federal laws. It also states the extent to which you will be liable as a result of damages that may occur while your product is being utilized, including the replacement policy for damaged disks. While the warranty is generally written in legal terms, you can write one without hiring a lawyer. Just read a few from other commercial software manuals and you'll get the idea. If your product is going to be sold through a major distributor, they will have their lawyer check it out anyway. Either way, it is a good idea to include such a statement with all programs you distribute, even on a local basis.

A legal copyright notice should be included on either the disclaimer page or the title page. An example of such a copyright notice is shown below.

© 1985 CompuTrain All Rights Reserved

Trademark and other credit notices are also generally included on the disclaimer page.

Title page

The title page should be attractive in order to motivate the user to read the rest of the manual. While there seems to be little standardization on the type of information to include, I recommend you at least include the following:

- *Main title*—This should be the same one you used on the computer disk so that the learner can associate the two pieces of courseware.
- *Company title or logo*—If you are going to produce more than one computer product, it is a good idea to establish a company identity. If you distribute through a regular company, they will place their title and/or logo on this page; but if you are an independent developer, it is a good idea to have your

title/logo present as well. You will never establish a reputation if you don't let people know who you are and what you have produced.

* *Copyright information*—If this is not included on the disclaimer page, definitely include it on the title page.
* *Company address and/or telephone number*—If this is likely to change during the life of the product, don't include it. Otherwise, do include it. It may bring you a few complaints, but it may also bring you increased sales from people passing the word on to colleagues and friends. A lot of good CBI software dies in the market because people forget where they purchased it. They can't purchase additional copies or recommend purchase to others.

Table of contents

No matter how short your user manual is going to be, you should include a table of contents that include chapter or section titles and subsection headings with their page numbers. Figure 9.1 shows one way to present a table of contents for a CBI manual. Notice the use of upper- and lowercase letters and spacing to highlight different levels. Using an outline style allows the user to scan down the page for the major section title, then to move in for the selection of the more specific subheading. The use of uppercase helps main headings stand out visually, which speeds up the scanning process.

Providing a tabbed edge like that shown in Figure 9.1 can also help speed up access to the relevant portions of the manual.

Preface

People don't want to waste a lot of time reading a manual that is not appropriate for them or that will not meet their immediate needs. The preface introduces the manual to readers. It should generally cover the following topics:

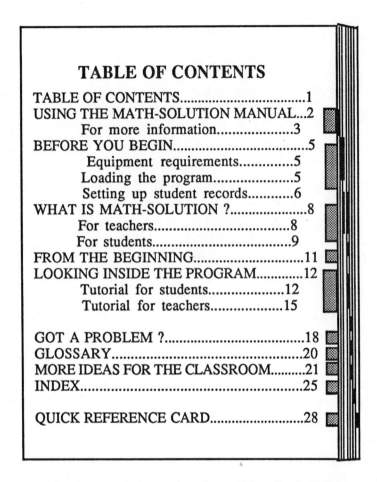

TABLE OF CONTENTS

Figure 9.1 Documentation table of contents

- *Audience*—who the manual is designed for and which parts should be read by which audience, i.e., teachers, students, parents, others.
- *Organization*—how the manual is organized and the approach the learner should take when using the manual.
- *Purpose*—what the manual is intended to provide and how it is to be used, i.e., as a reference guide, program supplement, teacher resource, etc.
- *Prerequisites*—what the reader of the manual should know

or do before reading the manual, and what other manuals the reader should have access to.

Introduction

The introductory page(s) should give the reader a concise overview of the manual and the related computer software. It should list the title of each piece of material (both printed and computer software) that is included in the courseware package. If more than one program is included on a disk, each program should be listed separately. If the main title for each piece does not effectively communicate the purpose of the material, a secondary descriptor should be added. For example, a title like "Constellation" does not tell much about the nature of a program. Adding the subtitle, or descriptor, "Locating constellations in the night sky," provides enough information for the reader to decide whether they are interested in reading more about this particular program.

The purpose for the introduction is to provide the reader with a short overview of each item included in the package. For CBI programs, in addition to the title, the following information could and should be included:

- *Objectives*—State the major objectives for each item included in the courseware package, including specific objectives for each computer program.
- *Program type*—List whether the item is a game, support booklet, tutorial, drill-and-practice, simulation, etc. Also answer the question, "How does it work?" If it's a simulation, what variables are manipulated and what is the outcome? How does it carry out the drill or tutorial?
- *Preparation*—State relevant knowledge and skills the learner needs in order to use the program effectively, e.g., reading level, math skills, motor skills, etc. This may also be expressed as a statement of the grade or learning level for whom the package was originally designed.
- *Descriptive overview*—Provide a one-paragraph overview of the item. The purpose is not to tell readers everything they

need or want to know about the item but to show its relevance to their needs in order to motivate them to seek out the program and the more detailed information provided elsewhere in the manual.

Equipment list

One of the first things a lot of people want to know about your program is what equipment they need to make it work. If not included in the introduction, this information should be included somewhere in the introductory pages.

Cookbook startup

Some readers don't have the patience to read through a user's manual before they start the program; others don't need much help. For this reason the introductory section of your manual should include a short, cookbook-type approach to getting started with the computer program. This portion of the manual usually contains lots of pictures and very few words. It shows the reader how to load the program into the disk drive, how to turn the computer and monitor on, what the first screen will look like, and what to do next. It may also include a short trouble-shooting section to answer the short-term question, "What do I do if my screen doesn't look like the one in the manual?" It doesn't go into a lot of detail on the inner workings of the program or management portions of the package.

9.3 OPERATING INSTRUCTIONS/EXPLANATION

The operating instructions or explanation make up the core of the manual. It may be approached from several different ways. For some complex drill-and-practice, problem solving, or simulation programs, a printed tutorial approach is necessary. For most programmed tutorials and simpler CBI programs, a more general explanation may be all that is required. Generally you will work with two major types of audience, that is, teachers and learners. Each has quite different needs, so you will probably have to provide two explanation sections, one tailored to each.

Tutorial approach

Many of the CBI programs you design will fall into the general category of a tutorial, so you already know that a tutorial should function like a one-on-one teaching-learning experience. When a CBI program is complex enough, or requires complex input/output procedures, it may be necessary to provide the user with a short tutorial on how to effectively utilize all of the program's options. Even with some computer based tutorial programs, the operation may be simple enough for the learner, but the management component, which is provided for the teacher, may require a tutorial to help teachers understand and utilize all of the various functions. In this situation only the teacher tutorial should be provided. The learner should be provided only a short program explanation.

What are the components of a good tutorial that is designed to teach program operation? First, turorials provided in user manuals should be kept as short and as simple as possible. They should get the user into the computer program quickly, and they should be presented visually as well as verbally. From the very beginning, users of the tutorial should be able to say, "That's just the way my screen looks."

Tutorials should:

- Guide the user step by step through the program.
- Show examples of what the screen should look like and what a typical interaction sequence might contain.
- Point out places in the program where common mistakes are made and show ways to avoid or get out of mistakes.
- Anticipate user questions and provide straightforward answers to specific problems.

- Explain what each step is intended to do.
- Explain the available options the user has at any given time and show how to access them.
- Be self-contained so that learners don't have to jump all over the manual or to other manuals to get necessary information.

All of the above should be provided in a logical order, preferably the order in which the user will go through the program. Future procedures should be included.

To be most effective, tutorials must provide practice sessions for the learner. Many tutorial users have difficulty coming up with the artificial data required for such practice sessions. The tutorial should provide sample exercise information to be typed in by the user. If the exercise data would normally have come from another program or outside source, such data files could be provided on a supplemental sample data disk provided with the courseware package.

Generally, tutorials included in user manuals are linear or sequential in nature, i.e., all learners go through the same material in the same order. Unlike the CBI program that you may be designing, it is not recommended that user manual tutorials utilize complex branching techniques. What is suggested is that the readers be provided some type of "tutorial map" that will help guide them to selected portions of the tutorial. If, for example, the reader already knows how to load a disk and start up the computer, what sections can they skip, and where in the tutorial should they start reading? If they only want to find out how to set up or enter a set of problems to be used in a drill and practice, which sections should they read? Providing a table of contents to the tutorial is one approach. Figure 9.2 shows a visual solution. By following the page numbers shown on each of the tracks illustrated in the flow chart, the learner can select the route through the tutorial that best meets their needs.

The normal flow of the tutorial should proceed from the basics of getting the program loaded and running on the computer and using the basic functions of the program to understanding how to use the detailed and optional functions.

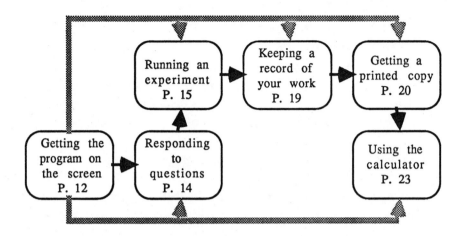

Figure 9.2   Tutorial content flow chart

The reader of the tutorial should be encouraged to be at the computer terminal while going through the tutorial; and each section of the tutorial should be correlated with what the learner will actually see on the screen. That's one reason it is advantageous to provide a sample exercise disk if outside data are required by the program.

Each section of the tutorial should contain the following subsections:

- *Purpose*—Each subsection should begin with a summary of what the reader will learn from going through that subsection. This gets the reader ready to learn, and it also alerts readers that, if they already know how to do what the subsection covers, they should move on to the next subsection.
- *User/computer interaction*—Shows the reader what the computer screen should look like, what actions the user should take, and what the computer should do as a consequence of the user's actions. Anticipate variations in computer systems. If the screen will look different depending on whether the reader is using a computer with an 80 column card or not, help the learner understand the difference so they won't

panic when their screen doesn't look exactly like the ones shown in the manual.

- *Warnings*—Anticipate problems and/or errors on the part of the user or the computer and tell the reader how to avoid or overcome such problems. Users often need to learn what to do if something goes wrong as much as they need to know what to do if everything works just right. Explain error messages that the learner may commonly encounter at various points in the program.

- *Helpful hints*—Users need to get in the habit of using some of the options you include in your program. Helpful hints remind readers that such options exist, in addition to the current topic of the tutorial. The subsection can also be used to show an example of how using the option would help the learner in the current situation or exercise. Remind readers about available help pages and show them how to access these pages from their current location in the program.

- *Keywords/Actions summary*—Readers will not remember everything you teach them. A summary at the end of each subsection will help reinforce the most important ideas covered in that subsection. It will also act as a quick reference for review purposes later. A similar summary or quick reference should be provided at the end of the tutorial, which covers and summarizes all the subsection summaries.

- *New vocabulary definitions*—Sometimes it is necessary to use jargon to get information across accurately and quickly. When a new vocabulary word is introduced in a tutorial, provide the reader with a short explanation, in their terms, of the meaning of the new word. It will mean more if you do it at the point where the word is used, rather than just provide a general glossary at the end of the manual and expect the learner to look up every word they don't understand.

When laying out your tutorial, use boldface headings to help the reader locate major sections so they can return to these sections later if necessary. Use pictures of the actual screens that the reader will be seeing, and other types of graphics to illustrate the relationships that exist between program parts.

Keep the tutorial subsections short. Apply the same guidelines that were suggested in an earlier chapter. People that use any part of your product should not be tied down for longer than 10 to 15 minutes without having a way to exit gracefully. Experience has shown that a user's ability to remember details drops off rapidly after about 15 minutes if they are not given a break in the routine. Such mental breaks should be encouraged. One way to provide such breaks is to encourage the reader to practice what they have already learned before going on. The fact that they are not learning anything new during this period seems to have almost as positive an effect as walking away from the entire tutorial for a short time.

Make sure you reward the reader for his/her efforts. We all enjoy a pat on the back now and then. A few words of praise at appropriate points in the tutorial will do a lot to motivate the reader to complete the entire tutorial.

Program explanation approach

Many CBI programs are relatively self-explanatory, and so they do not need all the effort that goes into a documentation tutorial. Even on the simplest programs, users need to be provided with some explanation of the purpose and functions provided by the program.

A program explanation should contain many of the same components present in the tutorial approach, leaving out the hand-holding which is characteristic of that approach. The explanation generally begins with a short overview of the system's requirements. It tells the user the brand and model of computer which is required, the required amount of memory, and what peripheral equipment the program may require, e.g., printer, light pen, extra disk drives, and so on.

The second thing that most program users would like to have available is a description of the learning environment in which they will be operating. A description of this environment includes a review of the general procedures and strategies that are used throughout the program, along with individual options that will be available to the user as he/she proceeds through the program. A short description should be provided for each lesson option which the learner can access through one of the program's menu frames, as well as a short description of each of the input/output functions which may be accessed through the keyboard or some other peripheral device.

The remainder of the program explanation section will generally be broken into two parts, one for the teacher's use, and one for the learner's use. The following are some of the topics that might be covered in the teacher's section:

- *Program design background*—During the process of developing your program you collected large amounts of information about the instructional needs, target audience, cost benefits, related materials, tasks, etc. In many cases, a summary of the essential parts of this information would be helpful to teachers in planning the integration of your program into other learning experiences.
- *Applied models*—If a nonstandard learning model or a simulation model was used in your program, the nature of the model should be explained. CBI simulation models are purported to be a mathematical or logical representation of the real world. Providing the teacher with a description of the model and basic assumptions underlying it, i.e., theoretical, research, statistical, philosophical, etc., will help the teacher accurately assess the possibilities and limitations of the model, and will help him/her explain to learners its accuracy and application in the real world.
- *Specific objectives*—In the preface section of the manual it was suggested that you provide all users with the general objectives of the program. Teachers may require more specific objectives in order to design tests and other follow-up activities.
- *Teacher options*—Many CBI programs provide the teacher with management options not generally available to the learner. These may include options like test item construc-

tion, reviewing student progress, assigning specific learning activities, and so on. A description and explanation of how to utilize each available option should be provided in this section.

- *Sample frames*—Provide a sampling of actual frames to help the teacher understand how the program operates and to allow the teacher to anticipate problems certain students might have in working with a particular program or frame design, e.g., physical and learning handicapped students.
- *Learning schedules*—Provide a typical schedule for the completion of various portions of the program. This will help the teacher plan and integrate your program into the total learning environment.
- *Implementation plan*—Provide a typical plan for implementing your program with related materials and activities.
- *Competency test items*—In CBI programs where the test items or simulation circumstances may be randomly drawn from a pool of items, the teacher should be provided a list of all available items. In other situations this information is not essential but is appreciated by many teachers.
- *Learner prerequisites*—The teacher needs to be informed of any specific prerequisites that the learner needs prior to entering the program. New terms that may be used in the program should be listed so that the teacher can make sure that all learners understand them prior to program entry.
- *Interaction strategy*—As discussed earlier, interaction is the key to the success of most CBI programs. Teachers should be informed and shown a typical interaction carried out by the learner and the computer.
- *Teaching/Learning strategy*—Teachers need to know more about the program than that it's a tutorial, a simulation, etc. They deserve a specific explanation of the particular teaching/learning strategy you have selected and some justification on your part of why you think your strategy is appropriate and effective for the particular subject matter.

Depending on the particular learner and/or learning situation, some of the information suggested above for the teacher might also be useful to the learner. In such cases it should be provided in an overlapping section of the manual. In addition to the background information just discussed, the student might need some of the following program explanation material which has been tailored to their particular interest and ability level:

- *Directions for program operation*—If operating the program requires more than simply placing the disk in the disk drive and turning on the computer, then a set of operating directions should be written for the learner. Even though the tutorial approach described earlier is not utilized, the explanation should be simple and friendly, showing examples of all of the major operations the learner will be required to perform.
- *Supplemental materials*—Reference materials and prerequisite information the learner needs prior to or during the program should be listed or provided.
- *Scoring/grading information*—If the computer is going to score, rate, or rank the student, the student should be informed of the basis for such grading.
- *Preferred learning strategy*—If there is a preferred learning strategy or sequence which the learner should use when going through your program, this should be pointed out.

9.4 REFERENCE SECTIONS

After the teacher or learner has been through your manual once, you can expect that most will use it for reference from then on. This means that they are looking up something specific because they are stumped and possibly even a bit frustrated. They certainly don't want to read pages and pages of commentary just to find which key to press to move on. The table of contents and the reference section should be used to eliminate this problem.

When organizing a reference section for your manual, put information about how to solve common problems before dealing with unusual or relatively unused options. As suggested earlier for the entire manual, organize the reference around the kind of questions your users will ask, i.e., "What action do I need to take now?" or "What function should I use to . . . ?" or "What tasks must I perform before . . . ?

Summaries

Summaries should be included in the reference section of the user manual if each of the previous sections have been summarized. Summaries help people do a quick review of what they have learned without having to search through a lot of information to find where they first learned it. They help synthesize and relate materials and information previously scattered through the pages of a tutorial or program explanation. They provide the user with a digested quick reference of the functions and procedures to be followed in program operation.

Summaries should not contain long explanations or references—the index should do this. Some of the best summaries are visual, not verbal. Diagrams, tables, and flow charts are effective ways of bringing together a lot of information into a minimum of space.

Another approach to summarizing information is the checklist or cookbook approach. Just as "Beat until fluffy" tells the experienced cook a great deal, "Option 1—Student Records" can remind an experienced program user about numerous details learned previously about a certain aspect of your program. Keywords have long been used to help people memorize complex operations. Lists of keywords are one of the most effective ways to help a user learn how to operate the complex procedures that may be called for in your program.

Glossary

The glossary defines words and commands that might be unfamiliar to the user but which are essential to understanding the program's operation or subject matter. Terms that are pure jargon should not be used in the program or documentation; therefore, there is no need to deal with them in the glossary. Avoid turning your glossary into a list of computer terminology. Only include words and commands you use in your program or in the related documentation and only words which give trouble to the normal users of your program.

A glossary should define terms, but is should be more than a dictionary of words. In application-oriented software like CBI programs, most of the words have some practical application. Trying to apply that practical application is usually why the user is looking up the word in the first place. For this reason, consider providing a short, simple example of that application as part of the word explanation. If the concept behind the word needs comment, advice, or warning in order to be properly applied, feel free to include this in your explanation as well.

If there are related terms that will help the user understand the term of immediate interest, the glossary can be used to refer the reader to them. Referring the reader to related terms precludes the duplication of long explanations. Cross-referencing helps clarify the difference between commonly confused terms, synonyms, and terms that encompass other terms.

Index

Building an index for your user manuals may be one of the most time-consuming aspects of the manual's development, but the long-term value of the manual can be judged by the quality of the index. Thanks to modern word-processing programs, indexing is not nearly the problem it used to be, since the computer can perform automatic word searches, if you can select the keywords you wish to include in your index.

Indexes are the tools you can use in a printed manual to make it random-accessible. It permits the reader to identify what topic they want to learn more about and then to go directly to the appropriate page(s). The index can also be thought of as a more complete table of contents. A quick scan through a well-designed index should tell your reader all the specific types of information your user manual contains.

Sometimes your reader doesn't know the appropriate term to use to access a certain piece of information. The index should be designed in such a way as to lead the reader from related terms to the more accurate, specific term. Indexes should therefore include more than just the words included in your glossary, maybe even more terms than are used directly in the manual itself. You want your indexes to be complete without becoming confounding. Too many terms may be as bad or worse than too few. It is better that a learner scan the index for the correct term than give up altogether just because it seems faster to scan the manual than to scan the index.

Which terms should you include in your index? Start by anticipating terms the reader will be looking for and the words that immediately come to mind for a given topic. If your reader has learned anything from your manual, the first topics that come to mind should be those covered by your glossary and the main headings within the manual itself. Every term that is used in either of these two ways should be listed in the index.

In addition to words included in the glossary and major topic headings, the index should include other commonly understood keywords which have been used in your program. Many of these may be subject matter words rather than computer-related words. If, as you read through your manual, certain words seem to have special meaning, i.e., they seem to stand out as you read them, consider including them in your index.

Once you build your main list of keywords taken directly from the manual, read and have others read through the list to see if there are commonly used synonyms, idioms, or related words that should be included with a direction to "see..." or "see also...." Keep in mind that the terms you use are not the only ones possible or correct. Make your index flexible enough to respect the terminology used by others.

When you have a list of keywords that you think is complete, begin to list the page numbers where each keyword or the related concept is discussed. Just because a word appears on a page doesn't always mean that page should be listed after the word. If looking up the word on a page doesn't add anything to the reader's understanding, don't include it.

After you list all the references to a term, look to see if you have terms that appear to have an excess number of references. These may be candidates for subdividing. For example, if your have lots of pages that discuss the topic "Scores," you might consider dividing the topic into scores-adding, scores-listing, scores-recording, etc.

You should also explore ways to group terms under a more significant main topic. For example, the terms "sedimentary" and "igneous" may be more easy to find if they are grouped under the general topic "rock" than if they are placed in their normal alphabetical position in the index.

There may be situations where terms should appear in more than one place in the index. There are also times when two-word terms or short phrases are more easily understood than single terms, e.g., setting up, saving it, "sodium—definition of," etc. If this will make the index and manual more usable as a reference manual, don't be afraid to do what is best for the reader.

The final index should appear in alphabetical order. The following is a typical index entry:

Name, Entering student 18,25,37–40

Quick-reference card

A quick-reference card should be designed to be torn out or copied from the user manual. Each user of the program should be able to have the quick-reference card next to the computer whenever they are using the program. It should not duplicate information shown on the computer screen but should act as a short reminder of options the learner has and the means for accessing each.

Options should be listed by function, not alphabetically. For example:

```
To Move Cursor press:
     Control-U ——— for Up
     Control-D ——— for Down
     Control-R ——— for Right
     Control-L ——— for Left
To Save press:
     Control-S ——— Save
     then Type File Name (10 letters or less)
     then Press RETURN
```

Quick-reference cards should contain any information a learner may have to look up over and over while running the program. Even though the quick-reference card is the most convenient way to look up information while a program is running, quick-reference cards do get lost. For this reason, it is a good idea to include the information contained on the quick-reference card on a help frame which is available within the program.

Appendices

Appendices are really a catch-all area for materials which are useful but not required for the successful operation of your program and which may be read or used by only a few of your program's users. Included in the appendices may be most, if not all, of the materials covered in the next section under the title, Support Materials. Portions of the technical documentation might also be included as an appendix if you feel it may be useful to a significant portion of your user population. In addition to the information suggested in these two sections, you might also consider including some of the following as appendices:

Sample program frames	Sample forms
Schematics	Techniques for programmers
Hardware modifications	Error-handling procedures
Program menus	Lesson flow charts
Program illustrations	Rarely used procedures

The reference section should provide a quick reference to all keyboard command function tables, input parameters, output formats, error messages and solutions. When multiple levels of program menus have been used, the reference section should reproduce each menu and show its relationship to lower-level menus.

9.5 SUPPORT MATERIALS

Since most CBI programs are written for use in a standard educational environment, it is not inappropriate to include some instructional support materials in your user manual. Sample handouts, pre-learning and follow-up activities, and text/evaluation materials are resources teachers appreciate finding in a courseware package. Because they are so appreciated they may help sell your package, and so are beneficial to you as well.

Instructional support materials which you may choose to include in your manual should be kept simple and relevant to the central purpose of the CBI program. Support materials should be included only if they will expand or reinforce a particular element of the courseware package. Among the support materials that might be considered relevant and appropriate for inclusion are:

- *Study worksheets*—If the learner is going to be required to reference large amounts of information presented by the CBI program, then a form for note-taking or recording might be provided. In addition to providing the learner with a take-away record of information learned, the worksheet can also provide the learner with a supplemental set of "homework" problems for those students needing more practice than the computer is set up to provide.
- *Score-keeping sheets*—If the program does not record the results of competency items for later review by the teacher, then the student should be provided a recording sheet so that he/she can manually record the information.
- *Quick-reference sheets*—Included here may be fact sheets on important pieces of information the learner will need to access in the process of using the program, e.g., math and statistics tables, vocabulary lists, conversion tables, etc.

- *Teacher answer keys*—The answer key should not be limited to just the answers to problems posed in the CBI and support materials. It should show the elements of the problem that are being dealt with so that the teacher will have some idea what is being asked of the learner. Labels that correspond to those used in the computer program should also be included on the answer key, so that teachers know which section of the program the problems relate to.
- *Background sheets*—Earlier in the book it was suggested that the computer not be used as an electronic page turner. If large amounts of background reading material are required before interactive programming is required, then that material should be provided in the form of a handout and not included in your program.
- *Simulation role cards*—In simulations where more than one user may actively participate individual role assignment cards can be provided. Then each "player" understands, without the rest of the group knowing, the basis for his/her part in the simulation.

In addition to support materials that aid in the instructional process, it is sometimes useful to include support materials that help the learner better operate the program itself. Included under this type of support materials might be such things as:

- *Care and handling instructions*—to teach and remind the learner of the proper procedures for using all of the courseware's components.
- *Error handling instructions*—usually provided in a two-column format, this support handout lists in one column the typical types of errors and error messages that learners are likely to encounter and in the opposite column a list of the solutions or ways to overcome the problem.
- *Equipment procedures*—may include a sheet that shows the learner how to load the diskette into a disk drive. If a modified keyboard is used by the program, a keyboard overlay

could be provided with the support materials so that the learner doesn't have to remember the function of each key.

9.6 TECHNICAL DOCUMENTATION

Technical documentation is not developed for the benefit of the normal CBI user audience, but is compiled for use by the technical personnel that will program, maintain, and/or modify your CBI courseware. For this reason it is generally not included in the general user manual discussed above. It is possible that this piece of documentation will not be provided for anyone except the technical personnel working with you, but this makes its careful design no less important.

The purpose of technical documentation is to provide programmers and other technical personnel with the information they need to program and make modifications on the CBI system you have designed. It therefore serves both a pre- and post-programming function. It should insure that all of the up-front design efforts you put into your program are properly carried out in the final programming process. It also should make it possible for you to easily revise the program and, where appropriate, for individual purchasers to modify and maintain it on their particular computer system.

A complete set of technical documentation would include all of the information you collected from the needs analysis that started the CBI design process (discussed in Chapter 1) through the writing of the program code and documentation, to the evaluation data that concludes and validates the process. A complete set of technical documentation should be maintained by you for future reference, but not all of this information is essential to the work to be performed by others. The documentation given to other technical personnel should provide them with the mechanism to quickly and easily obtain all the technical information they need to do their assigned task with a minimum of required reading and redundancy. Information included in the user manual should generally not be repeated in the technical documentation, although technical personnel should have access to the user manual. The following are some of the components of technical documentation which have been found to be most useful by outside technical personnel:

Application overview and procedural specifications

Before technical personnel get involved with the detailed, technical aspects of your program, they should be introduced to the general purpose and procedures the program is intended to fulfill. Unlike the user manual, computer jargon and technical terminology may be used to help describe the applications and procedures, if they make the explanation more concise and technically accurate.

Input/output requirements

The information that could be provided in this section documents the input and output requirement of the program and the internal variables which are used by the program. The section might include information on the following:

- A description and listing of the program's information input/ output requirements broken down according to information type, i.e., numeric, text/string, sound, graphic, etc., and information function.
- A description and listing of the program's operating input/ output procedures and requirements. This includes a listing of operating commands used by the program to control input, output, and peripheral devices, as well as a description of the keyboard and other control mechanisms which will be used by the end user, to access and control these devices and processes.
- A listing of variable labels used to store, manipulate, or out-

put information, along with an explanation of the function each serves in the program.

- A listing of constant labels along with the default value which the program establishes for each constant. If constants and variables have maximum and/or minimum value parameters within which they must function, such parameters should be documented in this section. The location in the program where the value of the constant is set should be included if modification of the value is possible.

- A description of external storage file specifications, including: file types (e.g., random access, sequential, etc.), file size, file labels, and record and field formats.

- A description of technical specification for interfacing various peripheral or accessory devices which might be used for the input or output of information. There is no need to duplicate the information provided in a technical manual that comes with a particular peripheral device such as a printer, but your technical specification should indicate the type of printer your program will work with and how and where those devices are accessed by the program. If special printer or peripheral device drivers are or can be used in conjunction with your program, a technical explanation on how to attach these drivers to the program would be appropriate in this section.

Program flow specification

This information should be designed to give technical personnel an overview of the flow of the program, and make explicit every single step involved as the program moves from one point to another. This section could include:

- *Flow diagrams*—These illustrate both the general and specific tracks individuals can follow as they proceed through the program. In the case of most CBI programs, diagrams should be included that illustrate flow through the instructional frames and interaction sequences, in addition to flow diagrams which illustrate the collection and management of learner data and setting up of file structures.

* *Menu specifications*—If menus and sub-menus are used to control the flow of the program for the end user, then a menu flow chart and composite description of all menus used in the program should be provided, along with an overview of the function and flow provided by each menu option.
* *Learning map diagrams*—As described in Chapter 2, these diagrams are designed to illustrate the sequence and flow of the instructional content without regard to the actual program flow.
* *Error handling procedures*—The messages and procedures used in handling user errors may be one of the most technically complex portions of a program. The procedures used should be carefully documented along with the program location of sub-procedures designed specifically to handle this component.
* *Program/code listing*—You may not want everyone to get their hands on a copy of your program code, but for those who have a need to know, it is an invaluable part of the technical documentation. Even if it is possible for technical personnel to list your program from the disk, it still saves a great deal of time if a printed copy is provided. Remark statements, i.e., comments and reminders which can be left in a program without affecting the execution of the program, should be liberally left in the program listing which is provided as a part of the technical documentation. To save memory, such remarks may be removed on the final version of the program provided to the user, but this valuable programming aid should not be lost for technical personnel who may need it later.
* *Equipment modification procedures*—When special interface boards or peripheral devices are used with a program, modifications on the computer or other devices have to be made, e.g., the shift key modification which used to be quite common on some earlier computers. Specific procedures for making such modifications should be included along with appropriate warnings on the danger of making such modifications.

Technical documentation, like user documentation, should not be cluttered with a lot of unnecessary information or technical jargon. It should be technical only in the sense that it provides more detailed information on a program's operation and the design procedures which led to the program's development. It allows the documentation writer to assume technical knowledge on the part of the reader which is not assumed with the normal user. But even the most technical person appreciates simple, straightforward, concise writing. Technical people rarely require added motivational materials. They come to the documentation with a need and their only real interest in reading the documentation is to find the answer to their need in the shortest, most precise, and accurate way possible.

Whether you are writing manuals designed for the novice user or for highly technical personnel, your documentation should be kept friendly, clear, concise, functional, and above all appropriate to the intended reader.

If you are not a good writer, or if you feel that you have too technical a background to write for nontechnical readers, or lack the technical background to write technical documentation, find someone else to write portions for you. Don't assume that you or anyone else will write a good set of documentation the first time through. Plan on writing and rewriting most sections. In between rewrites share the documentation with both technical and nontechnical friends, but above all find someone who has characteristics similar to your intended audience and share your documentation with them. Then be open to their criticism and suggestions. Ask them for help not only on the general content but on the style and even the way the index and other reference sections are structured.

9.7 SUMMARY

All CBI programs should be accompanied by some form of printed documentation. Depending on the nature of the program, the documentation may be as short as a single sheet or as large as a small book. Generally the documentation should be written for a nontechnical audience and, in the case of CBI programs, should be written for at least two major audiences, i.e., learners and teachers. The documentation should be organized and written around what the user will do or is expected to do with the program.

Documentation, which is written in the form of a user manual, normally contains:

- Introductory pages
- Operating instructions
- Reference sections
- Support materials
- Technical documentation

The introductory pages of the manual provide a disclaimer which states the rights and responsibilities of the program's owner and the copyright holder. The title page should contain the program's main title and important subtitles, copyright information, and company or personal ownership information.

The table of contents should provide rapid access to relevant sections, enabling the user to bypass sections that don't meet immediate needs. It should be designed around the kinds of questions average users ask.

The preface describes the intended audience, organization of the manual, purpose, and prerequisites for using the manual.

Introductory pages provide the reader a short overview of each item included in the package, including their objective, program type, necessary preparation, and general content. A listing of required equipment and supplies as a short how-to-get-started section could also be included in the introductory pages.

The operating instructions and explanation section should meet the needs of both the instructor and the learner. It can be written in one of three ways, i.e., as a tutorial, as a program explanation, or as a combination of both styles.

The tutorial approach is a step-by-step hand-holding approach where the user is led through the program's operation with short procedures and sample data. All of the major steps required for effective program operation are covered. Each section of the tutorial should provide: a statement of the section's purpose, a hands-on description of all user/computer interaction, warnings of potential problem areas, helpful hints, and a glossary of new terminology.

The program explanation approach lacks the hand-holding characteristic of the tutorial approach but provides most of the same information. It may also include sections dealing with: background on the program's design, applied models, specific performance objectives, teacher options, sample frames, recommended learning schedules, a recommended implementation plan, competency test items, learner prerequisites, interaction strategies, and teaching/learning strategies as well as additional material that may be of specific use to either a teacher or learner.

Reference sections provide a quick reference to all information contained in other sections of the manual. It may include summaries, a glossary of important terms, and an index to the manual. Every user manual should contain a quick-reference card, which can be torn out, and which contains any information that a learner or teacher may have to look up repeatedly while running the program.

Support materials include sample handouts, worksheets, and other instructional materials a teacher or learner can use to supplement the instruction provided by the CBI program.

Technical documentation is designed primarily for technical personnel who maintain and/or modify your courseware. It may contain a listing of the actual program code, the program's input/output requirements, program flow specifications, error handling procedures, and equipment modification procedures.

All sections of a program's documentation should contain and be written in a language and style appropriate to the intended reader.

9.8 ISSUES AND ACTIVITIES

1. Write a simple documentation tutorial to show someone how to load and start up any program disk. Have a friend

who has never worked with a computer try to start up the computer with just your written explanation. Evaluate the results.

2. Write an introductory section to a user manual for a new or existing CBI program.
3. Write operating instructions or a program explanation section to a user manual for a new or existing CBI program.
4. Design support material for a new or existing CBI program.
5. Design a quick-reference card for a new or existing CBI program.
6. Develop technical documentation for a new or existing CBI program.
7. Revise a poorly written user's manual following the guidelines provided in this chapter.

9.9 REFERENCES

Apple Computer. *The Software Portfolio*. Cupertino, CA: Author, 1982.

Brown, D. B., & Herbanek, J. A. *System Analysis for Application Software Design*. Oakland, CA: Holden-Day, 1984.

Control Data Education Company. *Author's Guide*. MA: Author, 1977.

Digital Equipment Corporation. *Introduction to Computer-Based Education*. Bedford, MA: Author, 1983.

Kelly, D. A. *Documenting Computer Application Systems*. New York: Petrocelli Books, 1983.

Minnesota Educational Computing Consortium. *Writing Support Materials for Instructional Computer Programs*. St. Paul, MN: Author, 1981.

Price, J. *How to Write a Computer Manual: A Handbook of Software Documentation*. Menlo Park, CA: Benjamin-Cummings, 1984.

Strunk, W., Jr., & White, E. B. *The Elements of Style*. New York: MacMillan, 1979.

Weiss, E. H. *How to Write a Usable User Manual*. Philadelphia: ISI Press, 1985.

Index